Killer
Pavement
Ahead

POEMS BY CHUCK TRIPI

Cover: "Fin" (hand-manipulated Polaroid SX-70 print) © Norma Bernstock

Author's Photo, Book Design: Barbara Tripi

ISBN 978-81-8253-639-5

First Edition: 2015

Rs. 200/-

Cyberwit.net

HIG 45 Kaushambi Kunj, Kalindipuram

Allahabad - 211011 (U.P.) India

http://www.cyberwit.net

Tel: +(91) 9415091004 +(91) (532) 2552257

E-mail: info@cyberwit.net

Printed at Repro India Limited.

For Mary Ellen, Debra, Mark, and Cindy

Killer Pavement Ahead

Acknowledgments

Exit 13 Magazine, "1941: Buddy Gets Over on Western Electric," "Uniondale"

Soundings East, "Preparing the Soil"

Saranac Review, "White Azaleas"

The Cape Rock, "Learning to Draw"

The Alembic, "The Boy in the Ocean," "Uncle Joe's Roadmaster"

Poet Lore, "Cold Stream Beer and Ice"

Voices From Here (The Paulinskill Poetry Project), "Willy Spinelli"

The Stillwater Review, "Ringer," "Elegy for the Oaks," "Teleology," "When I Was a Boy"

Juked Online, "Under Contrails"

Natural Bridge, "There in a Great Composure"

Quiddity, "Snow Men"

Poets from the Center (The Betty June Silconas Poetry Center), "Old Orchard Beach"

Limestone, "I Say I"

Freshwater, "1956," "Advice to Younger Men"

The GW Review, "The Big Empty"

Edison Literary Review, "Tail Fins," "Sharing Smoke"

Acknowledgments, continued...

Taj Mahal Review, "Dark Water," "As to My Flying Career"

Passager, "You Have to Dream an Easier Dream"

Ping Pong Magazine, "Killer Pavement Ahead"

Sonora Review, "Gone Away Too, the Wolf"

The Griffin Online, "My Story Is All I Have"

River Oak Review, "Reading Yeats While on Vacation"

Journal of New Jersey Poets, "Wall in the Woods"

Off Line (South Mountain Poets) "Dying"

Tiferet, "Andrew"

Poetry East, "Circles on the Delaware," "There Is an Eye in Me"

*   *   *

Sincerest thanks to Judith Christian, Adele Kenny, Elaine Koplow, Jean LeBlanc, Barbara Mossberg, Priscilla Orr, and Elizabeth Tripi.

CONTENTS

* * *

1941: Buddy Gets Over on Western Electric

Pistons to the muffler baffles, *Jesus did it sing.*
Springs, bolts and gaskets, every ring and gear
torn down, built up, handlebars to street; street
to handlebars, painted correctly in *Indian Red*—
the nineteen twenty-five Indian *Big Chief,* late
of the NYPD, cruising Astoria, surplus no more.
Not even a GED, but he feels like a machinist.
And there are jobs in Jersey City, and he knows
where the testing room is—the fix is in. Slicker
slapping in the crosswinds on the GWB, *you
can't even see,* but he finds it okay, skulks by
the processing station, writes just so in blue ink
on the back of his own application: *Candidate
testing room 310*; goes up like he owns the place,
goggles dangling from his neck. *The test is cake*
but it does, it really does make him a machinist.

Preparing the Soil

You need to make yourself a sifting frame
regardless of use or weather or grade.
Consider two-by-sixes for the box,
though any handy scraps of wood will do
if they are long and wide enough, and straight.
You want a temporary tool for this,
do not waste time in over-building it.
Just enough strength, ample capacity.

A finer mesh will make for longer work
without an added benefit. Use coarse.
You will need an application of straw,
salt hay to check erosion anyway.
Once the topsoil is delivered to you,
try to remember, as you shovel on,
the cost of bagged or presifted product,
how it might make you unnecessary.

Stamina grows as proper shovelfuls
go slipping down the taut, crossed-wire grid
with each increasingly perfect pitch,
the shovel slicing through the homely pile,
soil sliding away, rock-strikes on the frame.
Soon there is an endless rhythm to it,
shovel, throw and fall, shovel, throw and fall
and you are sleeping, shovel, throw and fall.

In the end you find the work was worth it.
You may keep the pretty, crafted things,
the amulets and arrowheads and coins
culled from your newly seed-receptive soil.
You dig a hole; give back the little bones.
You bury them with all the rocks and stones
you burnished on the tension of the screen
to mingle in the sweet, protective depth.

White Azaleas

This is my house. I scored the plywood and staked it in long curving forms from the sidewalk to the door. I spread the slates to look random. I mixed concrete in a perfect proportion and amount, poured it on crushed stone at just the right depth against heaving, pressed a new penny in every ten feet, a nineteen fifty-three. I made these steps. I poured this porch on rocks and sand, watered-in. I covered the front door in eight coats of marine varnish. The foundation plants in six inches of peat moss, and the three white oaks lining the street with Kentucky Blue Grass on the median, I did this. When winter is lingering, I go in April or May as it fits my whim, reach in among entangled branches with my eternal index finger and thumb, strip the dead oak leaves away; I am the one. I bring spring to the azaleas, I bring the sun.

Learning to Draw

A fat glowing orb in a field of blue—you want light.
Sunny things, flowing down golden through the color
wheel. Regular fields of grain. Put a few birds in, two
flicks of the wrist. Trees in a nice greensward. Signs
of an ancient hunger—lots of big apples, red and green.
Lines to resolve into people, regular shapes into homes
for them, settled onto the hill, in bright pastels. A road
coming down, dark into the outskirts of town. Multiply
streets, by cars and by drivers and days, times steeples
and schools. To dark, add light. Do not over-think it.

Six O'clock Whistle

You could lie in the grass all day staring up at the sky
or hang upside down over a split rail fence, gazing up
at the changing clouds—there is no job or time to keep.
The colors seem to come in single syllables until the sun
slants down in airlight blue and backscattering red,
a big surprise. Bill Spinelli whistles for his children—
dinnertime. Fingers to the corners of his mouth, chin
tucked in below his upper lip, he sends a mighty calling
out into the streets and yards to distances of sunlit boys.

The Boy in the Ocean

The first time I swam in the ocean,
what could I weigh, fifty pounds?
A tidal wave took me,
twirling the world,
putting my feet where my head was,
my head where my feet.
Gone from the air, breathing the brine,
I was watching the bottom go by and at once
I was standing, alone among swimmers,
coughing the taste of the salt and at sea.
Turning my back to the shore
I was instantly hiding,
making the gestures of splashing,
assuming the postures of glee.

Cold Stream Beer and Ice

Little more than a refrigerator door
behind a loading dock on Front Street,
just across from Cold Stream Bar and Grill,
the Manor Inn, the Cold Stream Liquor Store.
A man with frosty hair would bring the block
with ice tongs *older than you, Sonny.*

He'd *tunk* it down into a cardboard box
and halve the block in seconds with his pick,
tink it into glinting shards, looking
all the little while at you, make a lunge
and twirl his pick and holster it; go *Boo*!
In the yard next door was Cold Stream Fuel Oil;

you can picture "Cold Stream Coal and Ice"
across the panels on the wooden lorries
driven by the iceman, just a boy in the day,
charred and smudged, muscled with coal.
He's thinking of the stream, cold and wandering
through Barnum Woods, the Meadow Brook.

They never end, the rides we took, fat-wheeled
Schwinns along the parkway there. We opened it
before the cars, before they even painted lines,
the four Spinelli boys—Jimmy and Willy, Vinnie
on the handle bars, Jerry, and me—Uniondale
to Sunrise Highway, all the way to Freeport.

Fishing with Father

It cannot have happened this way: sun-blanched, striated boards,
rusted nail heads, bait boxes hung from corroded cleats, a dagger
pinning the scavenger fish to the dock, and you said nothing—
Why catch it again his only explanation. How many ways
in the tries of that fish, you start wondering, to escape, to go
deeper down, all the way down through the planks toward
even a scent of freedom, from the sky into the familiar bay?
In that killing array of undulations, each one is worse.
How many days, how many worlds, how much will,
how many more expeditions after a failure to put up a fight,
you are going to wonder for sixty-five years,
trying to catch it again, trying to save it.

Willy Spinelli

He could swim!
His arms would circle up and down
like sweep hands on electric clocks,
without a tic, no sign of work,
but glistening.
His father made him stop
the day he took a dare to go
a hundred times across the Jones Beach pool.
The challenge of that whistle
was the one thing Willy couldn't swim through.
We figured he could swim to England.
Really, in a way, he did:
he swam across the earth and wheat and corn to California,
where he swam his way through school for free.

Down in Sarasota fifteen years ago,
holding Willy's wallet, watch and sneakers in the dark,
sober, old enough to lose a little faith,
ashamed of my relief, I guessed I'd better hide it.
Defiant of nothing, confluent,
after gliding by the alligators in the river,
still, he was standing near me on the causeway
proffering a stone,
as if to ask if I recalled a game we played
across the sparkling channels,
swimming to the other side,
bringing something back:
Go, get me a rock.

Ringer

I lead the league in stepping out of the box, spitting on my hands,
falling over backwards after making a routine catch; I leave my
top two buttons open so my shirt says *Bra ves*, but this kid can hit.
I would say the words if I could think them—*galoot* or *lummox*—
palooka; he's got to be fifteen. He doesn't even go to our school,
but Mr. Fortunato really hates St. Raphael's. *Tough luck*, he says,
have a little charity—he is from our parish, that's close enough.

the ball is so bright
arcing up into the sky
as if cannon-shot
to Uniondale Avenue—
his joy running the bases

Finishing the Attic

You want an *Armstrong* ceiling of acoustic tile, stapled to spruce nailers.
Kentile flooring, stud plate to stud plate. Tongue and groove knotty pine
knee wall to vault, beaded or butterfly cut, with cove molding at the join.
Nail the subflooring boards on the bias against lateral drift, all the way
into the eaves, with a *Masonite* substrate in finished areas, tacked down
every six inches. The void between ceiling and floor joists, even aside
from the cold, will serve as a sound box or echo chamber. Insulate fully
with *Gold Bond* rock wool batts. In a bedroom over-and-under layout,
place the batts over a few inches of *Gold Bond* rock wool loose fill—
you will not want curious children, ears to the cold vinyl tiles, hearing
from above you the serial hatred and bitterness each night, becoming
in turns riveted, timid and terrified, indifferent, other, all gone away.

1954: Your Hit Parade

We're sitting in front of our Admiral TV with its upholstered speaker and cross-hatched mahogany molding, Mother with her tea, Sister and I with our cookies and stuffed animals. *That's Amore. Heart of My Heart* has the *Hit Paraders* in cave man suits. They conk the women on their heads and drag them away. *Man and Woman* is staged in a mock boxing ring. Gisele MacKenzie ends it with a fall to the mat, but it's from swooning. *Stranger in Paradise.* Russell Arms sings *Secret Love*—I don't know, the room is cold; I ask a silly question: *Would you do it again, marry Dad?* Just now, just exactly now, my sister's face—our mother, there in front of God and Snookie Lanson, Dorothy Collins and the *Hit Parade Dancers*, stops to think for a good long minute, maybe two; gives the wrong answer.

Special Delivery

My mother and my sister fidgeting
in late afternoon and poor boy
Johnny Parodziewski riding.
Refreshment, style and sustenance
a little after school, the coolest breeze
on Frank the butcher's yellow bike,
with Cold Stream Meats—cube steaks
and some olive loaf or chicken breasts
in its gigantic basket, *quart of rye*
and two packs Chesterfield.
Frank would get them
at the Cold Stream Liquor Store,
a loaf of bread a quart of milk
at Bohack's, just next door.

Chores at the End of the Season

Before the awning is unstrung
and furled into its unwieldy cylinder,
flopped in the basement as the furnace
starts to chug, before the naked pipes
galvanized against the weather
announce again the barren season
we love the encroaching chill.
How it settles in the spine for a while,
a little while. On the patio the cold
concrete has never seemed so hard.
The awning fringe still flutters,
beach towels flap against the wind.
We gather them in, wrap up a last time,
huddle under the picnic table, play dead.

Mom and Dad Go to Midnight Mass

It gets to be too much, all of this peace
on earth. All of the bells and good will,
Bing Crosby. Fighters get to fighting.
Dishes will fly through the air. Genius
too much tested gets to a story—how
his father left him, just a boy in need.
He had to be a man. Next Christmas,

he had to be a man, the one after that,
each strand of tinsel perfectly hung
to be perfectly put away—but they
are gone now. Sway and backbeat,
abandon and hope, *Jingle Bell Rock*—
windows frosted with fake snow, you
and your sister, dancing to the radio.

Uncle Joe's Roadmaster

Dynaflow transmission, eight throaty cylinders. You hear it coming halfway down the block, the fake exhaust ports gleaming, hood ornament a finned silver spike that could eviscerate an elephant. Good things on the way to you. The first water rocket and pup-tent, a silver dollar when you let go of his hand. And Bunny couldn't stand the way he slept on the floor snoring after arranging the shelves in the store all night, the way my father's sister was so all the time tricked-up, the way she smoked, the way she jumped in the pool with her clothes on, *the animal.* A trunk as big as your house—a plusher carpet, too.

Uniondale

Behind the café curtains from the street
on Walton Avenue it seems the houses
brim with every kind of light—glow
and heat and flickering, the come-ons
of otherness. Familial concord, unformed
zenwords—filial piety, right livelihood.
Mom and Dad calm, reading their mysteries
deep into evening, all of the kids tucked in.
At the curbs the tail-finned cars, the lawns
along the sidewalks darkened to obsidian—
night, the only way you will remember it.
Smoke from a copped cigarette, older boys
to buy the bottle for you on Front Street,
premixed, tang and afterglow, ready to go.

Bung

It means *ward-off* in tai chi, but I don't even know it. Bunny is smashed on manhattans when I get home from school, comes after me with her wooden-heeled shoe, and it just comes naturally. I'm sick of her little bunny shit; I won't let her hit me. I do *bung* and it near breaks her wrist. I call her *a witch and a bitch, a dandy little housekeeper*, play *The Great Grand Coulee Dam* over and over on a plastic kazoo, *Hobo's Meditation*.

Drinks at the Runway Inn

Mickey and Sylvia sing from the radio
flying across the room. *Love Is Strange*,
but no broken teeth. A little hole
in my lip, where the air fluttered
through with the Chesterfield smoke
not two hours later at the Runway Inn.
Just a boy and his Dad, a few beers—
reconciliation, manly understanding,
every third one free. Two knocks
on the bar by a rheumy old gent,
a new salutation, *Good luck, Men.*
Love is strange, it comes to me,
and delusion, pathology and hate.
In the book of unwritten poems,
I *see* it, fifty-six years late.

Giving Up

After the fighting a boy needs to walk, numb
through the streets of Uniondale. Harry Karp
will be open. On the back of the paper bag, he
teaches his tricks of addition to neighborhood
kids, sells you cigarettes—your father's brand.
At Vera and Danny's you spin on the stools
until ten, wondering about surrender, a way
to begin, a way back in. *Chesterfields.* The reek
of the foil, rasp and rush and bitterness, a long
glow and ash after a dozen matches in the wind
right there on Walton Avenue, brazen in front
of your father's house. From the street,
you peer in, showing yourself to the stars.

Bunny and Buddy

Dark traps, numb hearts—but it's not every day.
Sunlight on the asbestos siding. Out in the yard
after dawn with a Spalding High-Bounce Ball,
tunking it off the walls. Dew-soaked sneakers
on a sparkling lawn, a *spaldeen*. Numb-hearted
in sunlight—maybe a parent becomes like this.
And everyone leaves, and it all goes with you,
two bodies, one flesh. Father and Mother and
children and Uniondale, grass and asphalt—
Buddy and Bunny, two bodies, one flesh.

Under Contrails

My father is dying. He is hauling his life
like a wagon of stones up a mountain,
a frayed rope, an attenuated will,
into the comfort of less mind,
the solace of not wondering.

The name of the mountain escapes me,
the city nearby. To tell you the truth
I can hardly remember—a rental car away
from Seattle or Vancouver. Long roads,
lined with plowed snow, narrowing.

Bare-chested on a windy ledge, we stared.
In one direction for a thousand miles
the snow is a clean sheet of paper,
written with pines. Branches, all morning,
shed snow, returning to form, lightened.

Orphan

We know how it ends, just maybe not now—
a gurney floats down the hall, going away,
maybe forever. She says, eighty-three years
removed, *I'm tired of all this death.*
She says, *I never knew my mother.*

But it's pleasant when her husband lives,
even if a little cockeyed and strange.
We make a little party at the Mohawk House.
A thimble of wine, a twenty-six dollar steak,
the Boston cream pie—it takes her forever.

They took us to the lake, she says,
and then they disappeared. When Betty died
they said she was a saint. Everyone dies,
she says. She appreciates the company,
goes home to dream forgotten things.

Elegy for Father

Fast boys, fast cars, gone. They left you
Buddy Greatest Generation, sprinkler
and barbeque, badminton in the yard,
mimosa tree and bird house, five
hard missions at twenty-one,
ever more incendiary and glamorous.
Left you Buddy Five-Days, *Zippo*
and *Chesterfields*, can of *Schlitz*,
El Producto blunts, quick fists.
Farmed you out to die in mewling
histrionics, gasping at empty air
as if the first dying man on earth,
all of you gone, numb to the winds
over the scars of a fine, soft land.

There in a Great Composure

And when he died she stared out the window.
The old broken oak became beautiful. Swiftly
passed the days, and the days after that. Never
did the beauty of that broken tree leave her.
Its branches filled with crows. A lurid sky
behind it in winter, into which the noises
endlessly went, was empty of narrative,
held no particular epiphanies, only crows
and their caws, leafless branches, colors
of an approaching nighttime. To watch her
there in a great composure was to see it too
through the window, even if into a glare,
to hear it too as if the house's walls,
even as if the stones were utterly of air.

Snow Men

In a summer of hibiscus, blood red, white
and magenta, bees act up on the powdery cones.
But he hadn't seen much—of girls at the beach
in mind-altering suits, of unencumbered love,
heat. Even the winter goes by now in a fleeting
celebration, an adoring of the slantest light
making its glare on the bars along Lark Street.
At Washington Park, where the footprints stop,
the one pure thing, the last of the cigars again,
a civil dissipation, casting a shadow too.
Everything points into evening and whiskey,
not so bad. He stares into his own black eyes,
amazed to be alive, glad about love, sorry.
Snow men lead lives of quiet desperation,
they go to the grave, the cold still in them.

Old Orchard Beach

She wondered if they trucked it in, the sand,
as if these beaches were produced by man,
a sort of Disneyland made perfect
by this freezing rain. The billion bits, basalt
no longer stones, but flecks of black,
the broken shells, broken and broken
and broken again, the billion bits
gone small, they didn't truck it in.

She told me all about the wooden spoon,
the wooden heel at the end of a shoe
at the end of her mother's arm,
come crashing down upon her,
all about her father's pulverizing fist,
they didn't truck it in, the sand.
We wondered at the time it took
for stones to ripple in a wave

across the strand and settle
into drifts not to be taken again,
the tides when they turn dark,
the pounding surf disturbing
nothing ever again, and underneath
the sea, the sweet illuminations,
waving fronds, a rounding of stones,
a coast we thrill to even when it isn't cold.

I Say I

For every day of snow,
a day of snow.
I sleep in it now,
I and I.
Pink for a moment at dawn,
purple at evening, all through it,
I drink it, snow and snow.
I have a spine of it,
a spine of a column of ice,
a star on a star.
It warms me like stones,
a perfect, starry heat.
There is a moon of snow and I,
interstellar and irregular—
layers of powder,
granular pellets,
six feet deep of us.

1956

Different steel requires different ore. A Plymouth Belvedere
in cherry pink and apple blossom white, ready for summer,
needs airier ore. Air will make for fire, fire for strength—
it's in the way you shape it makes for speed. Let there be
no posts between the rolled-down windows. It should be
as if the highways will open upon your gaze, as if made
just for you, a few dear friends. *PowerFlite* transmission,
R, N, D, push-button easy, gliding to the beach.

The Big Empty

There's this red-faced killjoy in the gym,
braying his opinion and you can't believe
he still exists. There are cutters in line,
even on Sunday, engines of elbows
poking you aside, fights for a parking spot.
Bad weather on the megalithic holy days,
the vales of tears, the bliss to come
beyond imagining; there is enough,
it seems you are in luck. You can forget,
and this is how you know; you can go back,
truth to the contrary notwithstanding.
There's heaven on earth, perfect climates.
From more than this you can't return
remembering, or talking anyway; first loves,
there's an element of sunrise on the water,
calm or turbulence, a nice apartment, all
beyond the happy birthdays. After
having everything, enlightenment,
contentment, even after this
there's a big emptiness, you know?
There is here, this side of the Big Empty,
love and begetting, falling down, getting up,
pain and forgetting, from zero to now.

Tail Fins

We can see them crashing too, the stars
flung forever into nothingness—

the existential boot is pressing down
on our necks too. We gulp and strain
to get a breath—to walk a mile
without a water bottle scares us.

We long for all the things we hated,
another generation of frauds we are:

gold and white and tail-finned, it sits
at the curb, the Plymouth Fury
to a gallery of coos, gleaming
and still. It's a nineteen fifty-six,

iron and glass in sleek plasticity,
still, but it looks like it's moving.

Benignity

I insist upon it as so.
Even if I am its agency,
even if I am its wan
sputtering light
in a storefront alcove
on a Central Avenue
or an MLK in a tawdry part
of a tawdry town
a thousand miles away.
Even if I am the walker-by
wondering who left it on,
this arcing, flickering lamp,
even if in defiance
I am smoking again
this last of my cigars
glowing in the windowpane.
There is a chill,
but even the idling cars
at the light seem to have light,
even if traveling through,
even if ready to go in that long
slow rumble of the night.

If I Were a Stranger

If I were God, I would love you. What you have conquered
would be reckoned as conquerable. Where you have failed
I would reckon the obstacles formidable. If I were a Stranger
parked out front, my windows electrically down, smoking
in my Cadillac, I would while away hours hoping for you—
a metaphorical hearth, heat, rock & roll records, comfort.
From a swirl of Lucky Strikes, secret signs, a beneficent
mood. When I am dead, if consciousness remains, every
opposite reconciled, I will gaze on the colors of the lands,
listen for need in the mathematics of your music, intercede
for you. I will bend over backwards, see what I can do.

Dark Water

Minds as they rise and dwindle,
even the moon sits in darkness.
Three hundred sixty-five nights

oceans heave, black and deep,
a little spume in moonlight.
You are going away in the dark,

always hankering, secretly alone,
at home in the comfort of stars.
On the corner of Central and Lark

at the laundromat, my clothes
in the soap suds, dark, dark water,
vending machines, ends of a day.

Three hundred sixty-five nights,
light spilling out to the sidewalk.
Maybe as you die, the chemicals

release you. Sunlight on the water
somewhere else, birches, herons
on the lake, ravens in the pines.

You Have to Dream an Easier Dream

You need to land a Boeing Seven Fifty-Seven
on a Sussex County road—it seems to you
outsized and impossible, but need is need.
Squealing tires, a screech of scattering cars,
screamers young and old, stampeding—
genders and colors and creeds, running mad,
having a bad day. You have to avoid the stacks.
You have to somehow miss the light pole
with your lowered wing. Do not snap the wires;
stay between the fences and the barriers.
No, the engines cannot catch and spool again,
there is no fuel to fire them. Only now, do this:
let a dream go deeper. There is a sign ahead
you cannot read across a footbridge—walk to it.

As to My Flying Career

What's real? Not much. It was the same as you. In and out
of mind, real sometimes and sometimes not—winging it.
Along an arc of here and there, closer sometimes or farther
away, not really knowing. Fire warnings, mostly false.
The engine lights turn red, the bells all clang and clang,
their falsity a thing for much, much later if at all. Clogged
airspace, every weather, sudden onset rolls in capture mode.
Terminator shadow of the planet Earth at the end of the day,
sunset behind you. Clarity. It really is, the moon sometimes
a great, pearlescent pearl. Our voices travel, lonelier at night,
disembodied but they go direct, a crackle in starlight.

Killer Pavement Ahead

Wild Cartoons Attack Dog-walker.
Or as Smokey Robinson at lunch
in Motown hearing it wrong:
I Second that Emotion.
As when you only see *The lover*
in *The Plover Inn*, a past
or potency or act or hope,
loss, ache, want, a fear, hidden.
Even to absurdity or dreaminess,
resurfacing—*Milled Pavement
Ahead*, the way it only says
they are resurfacing the road,
expect a little inconvenience,
crazed raccoons, the usual delay.

Gone Away Too, the Wolf

When I was a boy, sleeping
next to the wall it amazed me,
the air and water and light of it.

My father is speaking, *the wolf
at the door,* always the wolf.
At school one winter

as I lay me down,
taking a look through the wall
I could see it, the wolf

among pines in the snow.
I worked too hard. My children
are gone, working too hard,

and gone away too, wolves,
need, a father. I see the air,
all of the parts and colors,

water and light. I look
at the people and see it,
all of the water and light.

My Story Is All I Have

Maybe Latin was the fog I landed in,
algebra the clear next day, things happen
like this. Still, for many years
I felt as if flung by time, out,
out from its hot center, by quake
or eruption, like a billion seeds
to the rich, turned earth,
somehow yearning
just to feed you and to set you free,
all of the metaphors, not just this one
mixed. It was the best I could do,
the best I could do it, one by one,
as rocks piled on a beam of light, removed.
I have felt this way too—deprived,
existential and afraid, but light—
light is my original condition,
I insist upon this, I remember it.

Family Reunion

She doesn't have a cocktail, but I have two, not so unusual.
It broke my heart, my sister goes on, *to have to drag him
to the dentist for the extractions*. She says the infections go
straight to the brain. *Or straight to the heart, it always gets
riskier*. He was getting a veteran's discount. *We're grateful
for that*, she says, meaning to say *we were*. Both parents are
dead now—neither of us has to rush. The clams in her soup
seem so tender, really, *an excellent lunch*. Each of us takes
the crème brûlée. Coffee, a third cup. We spend two more
hours not fighting, talking our mother and father up.

Elegy for the Oaks

Blue sky,
white clouds,
pine tops
where yesterday
the oaks came down.
None of the children
see it, they are gone.
Little but an icon now,
winged euonymus
in the yard,
burning bush
if you prefer.
The fire of it all,
ashes, yes, prefer.

Teleology

It's just a lie of self-deception
when I say I love a winter so.
Every night the sunset seems
to make the house a little colder.
Getting old, profligate with heat,
I cannot get too much of it—
two whiskeys are not nearly enough.

Every year the sun behind the hills
has sunk into a darker scenery
and through the barren trees
along the ridge its momentary flash
becomes a bit more blinding,
the neighbors' yards, the farms
across the hills more distant.

There is nothing for it but to know
this cold, the bones and light of it,
this loss after loss, this hard gift.
It's a word we have outlived, *telos*—
purpose, or *end*, this void pulling us in,
this merciful sloughing off, of memory
for hope, the agency of every heaven.

Orientation, Old School

My parents are scuffling in the breezeway. Poor Mr. G doesn't know if he should cross the street, or retreat, but I beat him to it. Every curse you've ever heard comes out of my mouth—by the time I reach the f-word I know where I am, straddling my father's hips and punching at him hard as I can, a start to the script of manhood. Once he throws me off of him I slip his giant fist and hear it crunch the shingle, cracking right through the asbestos. I must have been provoked. It's fifty years ago, and not a word of it was ever spoken.

There Is an Eye in Me

Even in the years of relative contentment,
reports *The New York Times*, suicide rates
among the cohort of my age start to climb
for a catalogue of obvious reasons. Pain,
dependence, loneliness, loss upon loss.

But there is at the center of me an eye.
As I was falling away to sleep last night
there was the old, inexplicable elation
I first experienced at survival school:
I refused for a reason I still do not know

to kill a trapped rabbit and was ordered
instead to swallow his eyeball whole,
which I did, it being a saline solution
and not too unusual a choice to make
by a jolly fire, with boiled onions soup.

On the palliative of a pine bough bed
I lay under my parachute dreaming
as with an animal eye still open in me
I looked up into the canopy of snow
and it was big, and forever, and good.

Luke and Janey

All of the kinds of light.
My father is cutting the grass
at the convent; I weed the beds.

Storm windows and screens, fall
and spring, swapping them out
in the basement—this holy house.

I practically sneak, back porch
to kitchen to stairs, down and up
for an afternoon, afraid to see in.

The names are so strange. Sister
Saint…Jerome, Jane Fidelis.
Teachers of mine, this light.

Come on, Janey, we're late,
my sixth says to my seventh
grade teacher, enlightening me.

Luke brings us lemonade.
She can punch a *spaldeen*
about a mile, I've seen it;

covers your cards at recess,
flip for flip. She can win
your whole stack, give

it all back with a laugh,
outrun the whole class.
Dark beauty, first love.

Agnes Joseph, quiet
light, dies in the fullness
of time, my father crying.

Reading Yeats While on Vacation

Among the circles on the water
in the cove off Wickford harbor
you can see the cordgrass twice.
A snowy egret with its whiteness
on the little bit of shore shows well
in the shadow of beach plum and pine,
one for real and one in mirror-water,
yellow-green and tan, blue-gray,
white with egret and cordgrass.
In the fall, I hear, from my generous,
accustomed host, things change.
Menhaden in thrashing thousands
trapped in the cove forever then—
the truth of it, striper and bluefish
in the absolute absence of reflection,
but, vacation ended, I will be gone.

Tenuous

Thin ice, the *comes and it goes* of it,
blink of an eye, all of the *here today*,
that's life, all of a *slender thread*.

Twenty-three years, a single cord,
four blades, maybe, spark plugs changed.
The one Briggs & Stratton still roars away

if there's fuel—I forgot that yesterday.
The way they panic, everybody now
over every little thing amuses me.

She flutters her wings once a year,
a heavenly butterfly over Mount Hood,
for a kalpa, wearing the mountain down.

Gills, we had, fins, tiny lumps for eyes.
Many kalpas, you and I, dear reader,
tenuous, crawling up out of the mud.

Wall in the Woods

The woods were not here,
these woods were not.
First was the clearing,
then was the building
(a satisfying year)
then was the wall,
a line of stacked field stones
the length of a pasture,
a splay of itself now.

There are lines kind of straight
in the wild, footings
for who knows what,
serial burgeonings,
deviated streams,
endings and flinches and starts.
Noises and silences,
the rain of dead branches
pecked from the trees.

Dying

Shrouded, and falling, unbeheld, no avuncular greeter,
no lights, into an endless pit the colors of, I swear to God,
Thomas Cole's *Expulsion from the Garden of Eden*, still me.

Unbeheld,
we are unbeheld,
like separate leaves
in the blur
of autumn winds.

Birds, falling from nests, invent wings. We want hope:
the birth canal, the colors remind me of the birth canal,
gristle and flesh, a coming alive, a changing of the mind.

Coppery green lichens,
tincture of rose in the stone.
A pathway in sunlight,
like everything else,
obvious, hidden.

Like rings around Saturn, of stars, the lights around Rome.
This living explosion. We leap from the sea, the sun and I,
from earth, the iris, the apple, the wheat, the sun, and I.

Picture a city
of time. The horns never stop.
I like a city, I like walking.
I go for my bread, for my fruit,
for my news, every single day.

Andrew

How easy it is to conflate the little stream
still going by the monastery where he lived
his canonical hours, for sixty-five years,
with the Paulinskill River, to see it as one,
his vespers and complines, his matins
and lauds, his twenty-five minutes a day
with Shakespeare and Francis Thompson.

We walked in the evening, aware of spring,
of the dying out of his confreres one by one,
peered a little into the infirmary window
at all of the inevitabilities, at those frail,
wasting men, and I asked him a question:
*Seventy monks when you came, only nine left,
does it trouble you, Andrew?* He said only *no*.

The river goes by the Millside Cafe in Lafayette
and is gone, making its way through concrete
bridge abutments, postulates and pine forests
to the Delaware. A table next to the window
can still be had most mornings at breakfast,
over the torrent where Andrew goes by now,
gone and becoming, becoming and gone.

Leafy Branches

Branches will grow from the stump
into leafy, actual trees.
If I could ask you to look
at the weeds that you poisoned
each year, at all of the hardy
resentment, I would. *Follow
the stem*, you always said,
*look at the seed upon seed
wasted under the maple trees.*
I would tell you *the fishes
are walking, nothing is wasted—
even a dead man cultivates virtue,
this is the afterlife, now.*

Circles on the Delaware

It is not that I am dead
that desolates me so.
It is that I am dead
without having seen.
Had I seen the circles,
I would have seen
no dying for the dead
but just a plummeting—
a bird with folded wings,
shooting down
more than falling.
Another swoops, another
and another crest on air.
From the shadows
on the Delaware
in fits and starts the shad
go darting, making circles too.

Physical Therapy

A broken spell.
It makes me feel a little old
when Kira brings the cane.
A prop. She's twirling it like a baton.
I think the words *the karmic engine.*
I think the words *spent fuel.*

Out the window, in the woods
the sawmill race, joined again
to the river. *Finished work.*
The saw was gone already
when I came here. Lucky Strikes,
rude old men in the lumberyard

remembering the turning blade—
bear tracks on the banks,
big as your head. I think the words
unnecessary reconciliations, hear
the clumsy footfalls of the therapist,
ache for Kira's little dancer steps.

Returning to Freeport

When a sad boy takes to the water
he feels as if home. Catastrophe,

drowning, even a small storm
seem remote, the sun barely up

over the inlet. He imagines
an endless peace in the vast

shining expanse before him, forever
gentle, the wavy cadences.

Quiet begins to feel familiar and close
as the sun comes up in the morning—

only light and another day,
a seaworthy Captain, how he knew

when the inlet swelled, to sail again
back into the bay.

Sharing Smoke

The man across the street calls me *Mister*,
just as I kept calling Mr. Homestead *Sir*
when he had the place, a slice of lakefront
where the birches dangle perfectly still
three decades later over their own image.
Even when we drank a Chivas Regal
carefully poured, his hands so palsied
the bottle clinked on the edge of the glass,
and smoked the sweet Havanas he would sneak
across from Toronto or Montreal, the smoke
billowing endlessly away,
it never occurred to me to call him *John*
or ask important questions while I watched
the littlest roll clouds clear the lowest ridge.

Thaw

Maybe you are not so old and love
has not become for you a catalogue
of chances never taken. Yesterday
the sunlight found me in a beach chair
out beside my shed, four layers deep
in two pairs of socks, with eight dollars
of cigar floating away. I was hiding
from my grandsons and my wife,
watching the smoke drifting out
over the snow and the pines
with the clouds to the Atlantic, thinking
of unopened shells and Gulf currents
in the satisfaction of a mild defiance,
wishing my little boys well.

Cavy and K-Boy

I get sad on Tuesdays, missing the boys. Cavy said *Hi*
over and over with a big smile; Kieran's yellow slicker on Second
and Forty-ninth. The way he kept himself from crying when I cut
his pancakes wrong at the Morningstar Cafe. The way he figured out
where the gummy bears are at the U.N. Deli: *Lift me up, Pop-Pop.*

> streaks of light
> in the rain
> white ducks
> on a blue lining
> hidden or clear
> gone or arising

Lifer

He made us cut through Woolworth's
when we worked the Mitchell Manor site
but never bought a thing.

It got a little hot sometimes for hacking at the brush
around the drainage sumps, and collegeboys will go too fast.
He taught us not to kill the job, how when you rush
it only gets the bosses wanting more.

The ladies in the yards behind the cyclone fence
were charmed the way he asked for water for his men,
and could you put a little lemon in?

Pepsi all around at Friedman's
when he put a flyer on a winning horse—

the gray-haired County Parks Department man, summer bronze.
Lucky I would think of him today from fifty years away,
standing here on Olsen's dock by Olsen's boat,

the mist of morning hovering, orange, umber maples,
golden birch reflecting by the shore—*buying it,*
so near to forgetting the small epicurean lifer,
the lunch counter at Woolworth's,

the smell of the doughnuts—
more joy to the cagey foreman
even than eating to collegeboys.

At the Rink

You are going around
and around on your wheels,
feeling like no one is watching—
you forget them.
Outside in the sun
after getting your shoes back
you still feel the height,
it's like missing a step.
The sidewalk's so funny
you could trip if you want to.
You go to the *Tivoli*
or *Moon-Glo* and after the movie
the sun is still there.
You forgot it.

Collette Rocchio

The better to believe, that spiders fly. A silver thread, Uniondale to the Kittatinny hills, *Angelus* chiming in the valleys. Tony Gaeta's girl—that womanhood becomes her though I haven't seen her in fifty years. We never could have dreamed a world so green and changed as this in a million years. She comes again on summer days, glassy contrails, firethorn to gable in the morning sun. How like entanglements of love from other decades, just a little tug. Silken filaments across my face, barely noticed, magic, brushed away.

Advice to Younger Men

Unlikely, that a naked woman in the desert
longs only for a place to lie down.
One in twenty thousand chances
she has waited there for you.
One in sixty thousand times desire knows
its destinations, gives itself direction
through the waves of heat arising
visible from those untouchable sands.
If you go, go quietly, bring water.
Bring a lasting shade, a cooler breeze.
If you should leave again, leave water.
Leave a lasting shade, a cooler breeze.
You will carry her with you.
Ten thousand years, the arid winds,
yet to blow the sands away.

Bunny's Bejeweled Pig

How everything is everything at once
or things turn quickly, or how you
get over it. It takes a while to make
a lovely sparkling pig. You buy it
dusty and unfinished, paint it pink
and gray, gouge a hundred little holes
with a little steel pick for a hundred
multicolored rhinestones, give it over
to a ten year old to take it to the kiln
at the hobby shop—sometimes things
are permanent. The way it *crunked*
on the steps after a small eternity
of falling into a silence—barely
out the door. Her voice a little bell
still telling me it's just a piece of clay,
the way she pulled me to her, how she
said *that's all it was, a piece of clay.*

When I Was a Boy

There was a star for every star.
For every ache and want
there was an ache and want.

I did not know the names yet
as I lay on the basement floor,
shot by enemies whose hats,

black or white, told everything.
Outside in the yard, I lay still,
imagining my own amazing death.

There were violent, Oedipal dreams.
I did not know the names yet, stars
or aches or wants or dreams.

There was Lollypop Farm, way out
on the Island, a ride on the little train.
Yesterday our grandson ran and ran,

he laughed and laughed in Central Park,
the little anarchist, going in the exit,
out the entrance of the Tropics House.

He shouts them out, the names of planets
or the numbers or the letters as he goes—
things get better, I wanted you to know.

About the Author

Chuck Tripi appears extensively in literary publications, including *Boston Review, Poet Lore, Natural Bridge, Hayden's Ferry Review,* and *Spillway.* His previous collection is *Carlo and Sophia*, a Cyberwit best seller.
A retired airline pilot, he is founding partner of The Paulinskill Poetry Project, a boutique press and community resource for poets of the upper Delaware River region, USA.

CRISTAL QUEBRADO

Viacrucis Poético

Jorge F. García-Samartín

Ilustración de portada:
María Luisa García Samartín

Prólogo poético
Ana Lorite Sánchez

Prólogo religioso:
Chus Villarroel O.P.

2021

"Estad alegres porque vuestros nombres están escritos en el Cielo"
(Evangelio según San Lucas 10, 20)

DEDICATORIAS

A los que 144 000 que lean algun verso de este Viacrucis

Al hogar de Nazaret, a los abrazos silenciosos de la Virgen, a San José enseñando al Niño como flecta la madera: A mis inigualables padres.

Al Bautista, y sus ardientes proclamas en la orilla del Jordán: A Santiago, con su pasión dialéctica, su sabiduría y su rechazo de toda autoridad injusta. Menos mal que tienes bastante más sentido estético y no vistes de camello.

Al oasis de dulzura que se encierra en cada uno de los capullos de la flor que es Santa Teresita: a María Luisa, una alegría viva y colorida y a su particular mirada penetrante sobre el mundo.

A mis abuelos:

A Moisés, en sus cuarenta años de camino por el desierto: A mi abuelo Paco, siempre andando, entre la plaza y la farmacia.

A santa Hildegarda, con autoridad sobre papas y reyes y fundadora de la botánica: A mi abuela Gloria, en la trastienda de la farmacia.

Al Padre Pío, que tenía el don de la bilocación: A mi abuelo Avelino que, aunque no se biloca, ha recorrido el mundo entero caminando a velocidades inalcanzables.

A Santa Teresa, que encontraba a Dios entre pucheros y dolores y es patrona de las Letras. A mi abuela Marga, que me inculcó el amor a la poesía y por cuyos ojos se extiende toda la Meseta castellana.

A las doce tribus de Israel y los doce brazos de una menorá; a los doce apóstoles, a los primeros doce que leyeron este texto:

A Pedro, cabeza de la Iglesia, enérgico y siempre vuelto a Cristo: A Don Enrique, un fiat permanente (incluso a lo más loco) que, como el mejor de los líderes no puede dejar de ponerse el último.

A Santiago, gracias al cual llegó el Evangelio a nuestras tierras: A Javi, por cuyas venas circulan las mejores virtudes hispanas: amistad, valentía, buen humor, optimismo, calma…

Al discípulo que Jesús amaba y que rezuma alegría en todo lo que escribe: A Ignacio, siempre sonriente y afectuoso, siempre creativo, siempre fiel hasta el final.

A Andrés, que se puso a hablar con el muchacho de los panes y los peces: A Edu, que habla con todo el que se le cruza y cuyo coche nos ha dado vida a muchas más de 5000 personas

A Felipe, que habló con griegos, samaritanos y etíopes (aunque cuando hablaba con Cristo, metía la pata): A José, nuestro guía inigualable en el extranjero y cuyas liadas (pocas) son tan buenas como sus muchos chistes

A Bartolomé, mirado ya debajo de la higuera: A Maca, vigilada desde siempre por Cristo (y por uno de sus ángeles) y ahora que se ha dado cuenta, se deja la piel por Él, aunque no literalmente como el apóstol.

A Mateo, en el mostrador de los impuestos: A Pilar, que, como Santa Teresa, sueña con los pies en la tierra, que corta nuestros derroches mientras negocia contratos imposibles, que es a un tiempo Quijote y Sancho Panza.

A Tomás, sincero y espontáneo, cuyas preguntas le arrancaron a Cristo su bella confesión como «Camino, Verdad y Vida»: A María Zavala, que mete a diario sus dedos en la carne de Cristo y nos enseña que soñar es quedarse corto.

A Santiago Alfeo, cuya carta es un modelo de liderazgo, mano izquierda y cultura. A Almu, que, además de poseer esas tres virtudes en grado sumo, tiene siempre la sonrisa que le falta al autor de la Epístola.

A Simón, que comparte con San José el privilegio del silencio evangélico: A María Lanzuela, discreta, pero con la pasión de los zelotes, capaz de ir a la tele o a las instituciones a luchar por lo que importa.

A Judas Tadeo, que en la Última Cena desea de corazón que Jesús se manifieste al mundo: A María Gallo, cuya inigualable labor en redes lleva a Cristo a todos los hombres.

A Matías, escogido por sorteo: a Diego, guiado desde siempre, aún sin saberlo, elegido para convertirse, con corazón enamorado, en santo en el día a día.

A Tobías y Sara, que saben confiar y hacen de la vida una aventura fascinante: A Pastor y Pati, de cuyas manos nacen maderas imposibles, ilustraciones vivas y oraciones de mágico lenguaje.

A San Juan XXIII, bondadoso como el padre del Hijo Pródigo pero valiente impulsor del Concilio (y con mucho sentido del humor): A Sergio Blanco, gracias por tener la valentía de *aggiornar* lo que hace falta y por tu día a día basado en mejorar la vida a los demás.

Al etíope que se encontró con Felipe en medio del desierto y acabó siendo bautizado: A Chini, que aprendió en una cena de la existencia de este libro y por cuya ilusión le prometí esta dedicatoria.

A Ana, la profetisa de Fanuel, a la que los necios tomaron en el templo por loca: A Ana Lorite, que también es profeta y predijo que un día escribiría un libro.

A la reina Ester, que estuvo dispuesta a morir por su pueblo: A Mar, que dirige con espíritu materno todo lo que se la ponga delante.

A los magos de Oriente que leían en las estrellas: A las profes de Lengua y los secretos de las letras que me enseñaron. A Sara, siempre fecunda en conocimientos.

A San Pablo, universal, enérgico e incomprendido: A Chus, que, aunque puede gloriarse en todo solo confía en el Cristo escandaloso y necio que predica. A su comitiva: Aquila, Priscila, Tito, Timoteo, Lucas, Bernabé…

Al rey David, el estratega cuyos Salmos encierran bellísimas alabanzas llenas de Sabiduría: A Don Jesús, cuya generosidad con las palabras provoca miles de encuentros con Cristo cada día.

A los lugares visitados por San Pablo: A los que me han ido acompañando por el camino de la vida:

Al desierto silencioso de Arabia, primera etapa, tan fundamental como desconocida: A Notre-Dame de Vie, donde aprendimos a ver a Dios y descubrimos que nuestra vocación es el Amor.

A la elegante ciudad de Antioquía, recta, fiel y cumplidora: A Santa María de Caná, abajo y arriba.

A Galacia, oasis cuando estaba enfermo: A la Capilla, abierta 24/7, y todos sus integrantes, un único cuerpo.

A Filipos, primer baluarte cuando llega a Europa, sostén a lo largo de toda su vida: Al Ker, con su Síntique y su Evodia, merecedor de la misma ristra de agradecimientos, «testigo es Dios de mi aprecio por vosotros».

A Tesalónica, donde aprendió a trabajar para no ser gravoso a nadie: a todos los que cada día me han enseñado cosas nuevas–amigos, desconocidos y profesores–. Gracias AwA por enseñarme a maquetar.

A Corinto, espontánea y colorida, a la que desnuda su alma: A los del cole, que me conocen desde siempre, a esa mezcla tan viva como a veces explosiva, que es imposible olvidar.

A Roma, que se sabe salvada gratuitamente en Cristo: A Maranatha, sin palabras, con gemidos inefables.

PRÓLOGO POÉTICO

por Ana Lorite Sánchez

Es poco frecuente y raro que regrese un ex–alumno ingeniero a la par que poeta. Más raro aún, que su primer libro, en los tiempos que corren, sea un Viacrucis. Es vergonzoso que a su antigua profesora le falten datos para comprender los versos de su alumno–su muy leído alumno

Se me acumulan los profetas, –Jeremías, Isaías, Abraham–, los sacerdotes–Aarón, Melquisedec–, los monarcas–Roboam, Saúl, David–, las mujeres–Gómer, Evodia, Síntique–, a Bartolomé lo nombra Natanael, al demonio, Asmodeo. Damasco y Malta son San Pablo, Umbría San Francisco y Toulouse, Santo Domingo de Guzmán. Un ascensor es Santa Teresita. El joven rico y Epulón comparten estrofa

No puedo remediar ser profesora. Necesito guía de lectura con mapa y cronología desde el Antiguo Testamento hasta el siglo XX para emocionarme aún más y más tranquila con este maravilloso libro, de cuyas estaciones elijo la novena y la décima.

Me hubiera gustado escribir a mí alguno de tus preciosos versos. La décima y novena estación, ya desnudas de datos son sobrecogedoras, qué emoción, Jorge, qué alma tan preciosa es capaz de escribir unos versos tan profundos. Leo en tus palabras un alma muy apasionada, capaz de sentimientos vigorosos, varoniles y valientes.

Pozuelo de Alarcón, 25 de febrero de 2021

PRÓLOGO RELIGIOSO

por Chus Villarroel O.P.

Me siento feliz al ver cómo el impulso poético de un joven de estos tiempos, casi niño todavía, escoge la ilusión de la fe para desahogarse. No es normal pero en este caso es muy real. Jorge lo aprendió desde niño, mamó la trascendencia en su propio hogar, el veneno ideológico no penetró en las venas de su alma porque sus padres han sabido estar. No, no es ningún espécimen de museo. Ha entrado en la vida, en los estudios, en la universidad, como cualquier otro, pero con los ojos aclarados, la mente despierta y el corazón a la búsqueda de todo lo bello.

Un viacrucis. Dios mío, ¿qué es eso? Con la lectura de las estaciones, el lector se dará cuenta que este chico ha tenido un encuentro con Cristo. Ese tú a tú con el Señor Resucitado le permite hablar de la pasión sin acritud, sin crispación y rebeldía, sin protestar porque el mundo sea el que es, cosa tan propia de su edad. La mayoría de los jóvenes si no se apuntan a la resistencia no tienen nada que decir porque su alma está seca por falta de corazón. Agradezco a Jorge que se salga de los esquemas predeterminados que todo el mundo espera al conocer su edad.

Las imágenes poéticas con las que se expresa son muy fenoménicas, poco esenciales. Es el kairós y la percepción de un segundo. Merece la pena releer el viacrucis más de una vez. Son imágines suyas, personales, difícilmente apropiables por otras personas. Es una pintura abstracta donde cada uno puede poner lo que quiera:

Sécame Madre las lágrimas
con tus caricias de lino, tu olor a rosa,
con el manto que curaba en las aristas nazarenas
mis rodillas de niño ilusionado.

Es la cuarta estación, el encuentro con María, su madre. En el momento de la tragedia los dos recuerdan para darse ánimos los días felices del hogar de Nazaret. Su vida de fe hará que ambos lleguen a la cumbre del Calvario y suceda la nueva creación.

Solo me resta desear a este viacrucis la mejor andadura. Si decimos que el mundo está mal debemos tener presente que el Espíritu Santo ha dicho: ¿Qué es lo que vence al mundo? La fe es lo único que vencerá. Y añade Jesús: No tengáis miedo, yo he vencido al mundo. El Viacrucis es la prueba de que el Resucitado ha vencido al mundo.

Madrid, 21 de febrero de 2021

Cristal Quebrado nace la mañana del martes 10 de marzo de 2020. Con la suspensión de clases previstas para el día siguiente y el confinamiento que nadie quería mirar de frente en vista de todos, Don Enrique nos aconsejó aprovechar las circunstancias para hacer algo «especial y diferente». En mi caso, fue la poesía.

Mis inicios poéticos no fueron nada extraordinario: como todos, empecé leyendo a Bécquer y pasé después a la sencillez profunda de Machado. A lo largo del camino me han acompañado distintos actores: la elegancia de Aleixandre, el eclecticismo de Gerardo Diego, el optimismo de Salinas y Guillén, ha habitado en mí el olvido…Me fascina–quizás demasiado–las metáforas y la complejidad que ocultan imágenes como las de Pere Gimferrer.

Para mí, un poemario es como un álbum de fotos en que el paso de las páginas nos lleva al lugar de nuestro interior donde se esconde la felicidad. Las imágenes poéticas, como las físicas, encierran algo más que su significado, nos hacen experimentar de nuevo vivencias que tenemos tan arraigadas como aletargadas. La poesía no son solo palabras, es la expresión de un misterio, el misterio de la complejidad humana, de todo aquello que nos recorre sin que prácticamente podamos controlarlo.

Y en medio de ese misterio, lo divino. Pero la persona de Jesús de Nazaret excede por mucho un planteamiento convencinal. A los cristianos se nos ha olvidado que Cristo, además de Dios, fue perfecto hombre. No la caricatura de un sabio ni un guerrillero sin personalidad. Hemos relegado a una estampita con tres dedos en alto la personalidad de quien tuvo miedo y rio, comió

y enfermó, tembló y amó. En los versos de las quince estaciones he intentado plasmar una psicología real, rica y humana, que podría ser la de cualquiera de nosotros.

Su sufrimiento es el de todos los hombres: las enfermedades, la angustia existencial, el miedo al futuro, la desazón están presentes pues, de otro modo, no habría sido redimidas. El Viacrucis engancha así también con el tiempo en el que ha sido gestado, escrito y revisado, en medio de la terrible desolación del Covid-19. Lo que empezó siendo un manuscrito de veinte páginas en la Semana Santa de 2020 ha acabado publicado por el impulso de mi madre.

Abundan las alusiones bíblicas y las palabras empolvadas por la historia. Soy tímido y me da vergüenza escribir, lo oculto todo. En mi defensa diré que nada une más a dos personas que la existencia de referencias comunes, algo que intento establecer en mis poemas y cuyo papel lo cumplen aquí los personajes del Antiguo y Nuevo Testamento. Siguiendo consejos valiosos, he añadido pequeñas explicaciones que intentan poner algo de luz sobre los versos.

Sea como sea, espero que lo disfrutes o que, al menos, la poesía haga revivir en ti el fuego de recuerdos olvidados y si eres creyente, que te sirva de provecho.

VIACRUCIS

Al principio de cada estación se reza:
Te adoramos Cristo y te bendecimos
Que por tu Santa Cruz redimiste al Mundo

Y al final:
Señor pequé
Ten piedad y misericordia de mí

Pueden añadirse
Padrenuestro, Avemaría y Gloria.

Oración Inicial

Entre poesía y salmo

Oh Dios, que quisiste redimir a tus hijos
con la sangre de tu Hijo,
que sufrió en su cuerpo de carne,
mortal y débil como el nuestro,
el odio, el desprecio, la enfermedad y la muerte,
todo lo que habrían de sufrir los nuestros,
haz que la oración del presente Viacrucis
permita encontrarnos con Él,
el único justo,
cara a cara,
con su Humanidad, salvífica y sanadora
con su pobreza extrema,
su misericordia sin límites
y poder entrar así
en el misterio profundo de su Pasión.
Por Jesucristo Nuestro Señor,
que vive y reina contigo
y el Espíritu Santo,
por los siglos de los siglos
Amén

ORACIÓN FINAL

Entre poesía y salmo

Oh Cristo Jesús,
ahora que hemos experimentado
tu entrega sin límite
por Amor hacia nosotros,
y descubierto que eres Tú
la única vía para llegar al Padre,
concédenos que, al clarear ya el día de la Pascua,
vivamos en nosotros
la alegría de tu gratuita salvación,
Tú, que vives y reinas
y eres Dios, con el Espíritu Santo,
por los siglos de los siglos
Amén,

JESÚS CONDENADO A MUERTE

Donde Jesús, humano, tiene miedo

La escala del Pretorio sabía
a beso manchado en plata, a soberbia,
al perfeccionismo helado de una clepsidra de metal.
Amanece naranja y huele a miedo,
Jerusalén es Babilonia
y tengo vértigo. La sed me pega la lengua al paladar
«Aquí está el hombre». «Sobre nosotros su sangre»

¿Quiénes son y por qué gritan,
por qué tiemblan mis pies, se encogen mis entrañas?
Viscosa nube verde de terror amargo,
son miradas que no entienden,
que han cambiado su lepra por veneno
pero son también ovejas mías.

El agua desparrama una sentencia fría,
firme Pilato, entre sus manos el Leto y de su voz,
una única palabra.

Miedo.
Miedo en los fariseos, que edificaron su casa en el desierto de la
Ley,
en las palomas sin nido de la noche
en la estrenada libertad de Barrabás;
y en mi sangrienta faz, sembrada de atuendos
y sin final torturas
absorbe, de los siglos el pavor
una nariz tallada de saliva

Abrazarán mis manos el gemido
de la escala del Pretorio y su sabor a pánico.
Yo también exhalo miedo.

JESÚS CONDENADO A MUERTE

Donde Jesús, humano, tiene miedo

Un escenario grecorromano encuadra la primera de las estaciones: en un escenario que parece una tragedia ateniense, no es la divinidad la que castiga, sino la castigada. Tres son los miedos que brotan, chocan y confluyen: el de los judíos, que han encorsetado tanto su vida que no dejan hueco a la novedad del Evangelio, el las «palomas sin nido», los apóstoles débiles, desorientados y «mutilados» y el de Pilato, temeroso de ver caer el orden establecido. El miedo de Cristo los recoge todos.

◊ La clepsidra, el agua fría, la escalera del Pretorio (aún venerada frente a San Juan de Letrán) son elementos de este escenario de tragedia clásica.

◊ El verde es el color en Lorca de la muerte.

◊ «Han cambiado su lepra por veneno» evoca todos los curados que alabaron al Mesías en su poder, pero no aceptan su debilidad y quieren condenarlo.

◊ «Son también ovejas mías» es una clara referencia al discurso del Buen Pastor (Jn 10, 9-16).

◊ Las «palomas sin nido» recuerda las palabras de Jesús en Mt 8, 20-22, que dicen que los que le siguen viven sin seguridades humanas.La escalera del Pretorio, o Scala Santa se venera en Roma, en frente de San Juan de Letrán. No escapa del turismo de masas de toda la Ciudad Eterna pero, al menos, está consagrada a la oración.

◊ «Jerusalén es Babilonia». Babilonia es, en el Apocalipsis, el símbolo del Anticristo. La Ciudad Santa se ha mimetizado con el mal. Porque nada es bueno fuera de Cristo (Mt 19,7).

◊ A Cristo «la sed le pega la lengua al paladar». Es una evocación del Salmo 136, que llora la destrucción de Jerusalén. Jesucristo llora aquí, como ya hizo en Lc 19,41-44, la soberbia de una ciudad que no quiere acoger su salvación.

◊ Pilato lava sus manos en el Lete, uno de los cuatro ríos del inframundo griego. Es el río del olvido. El gobernador quiere olvidar que ha condenado a un hombre inocente.

◊ La sentencia de muerte, «una única palabra» no se escribe: no hay hueco para oírla, suavemente pronunciada. Sólo se oye miedo: el de la multitud, el de Pilato y el de Cristo, que los abarca todos.

JESÚS CARGA CON LA CRUZ

Donde Jesús es el artesano que talla nuestras vidas, el alfarero del profeta Jeremías

Desde pequeño he conocido la madera
y modelado el barro;
la piedra, la montaña, el céfiro,
y he escuchado en los recodos
la voz de nuestros padres, a Isaías exultante.

Ni sus razones ni su odio, no entiendo
su grito en mis abscesos, mi cabeza rota.
quiero madera o la muerte,
besar sus nudos rugosos
quiero quemar de amor mis entrañas,

beber tu aliento de pecado: entrégame tu vida,
madera en movimiento torpe,
no me basta tu viruta,
te quiero a ti que eres viruta..

Déjame arrancarte tu aspereza con mis uñas
tornaré de haya tu color de arce
con mis gotas.
Quebraré contigo en puntas dolorosas
en imposibles formas, retorcidas brechas.

Ya está aquí la siega, brillan sus aceros,
un granero de amor y nuestros vientos
empapados al perfume del olivo.
Ceniza consumida por el fuego,
costuras de un mosaico colorido.
Y con el polvo en tus entrañas
un hombre nuevo de mi soplo:
madera de ebanista, negra de los Cantares.

JESÚS CARGA CON LA CRUZ

Donde Jesús es el artesano que talla nuestras vidas, el alfarero del profeta Jeremías

La cruz es inherente a la condición humana. Para Frankl, «vivir es sufrir, sobrevivir es hallarle sentido al sufrimiento». En la Pasión, Muerte y Resurrección, los cristianos podemos encontrar el sentido. Jesucristo tomó por nosotros nuestros dolores y los hizo suyos. Su carne fue el campo de batalla en el que lucharon, concretos, cada uno de los males que nos acechan.

Este poema es una vuelta a la infancia, al despertar a la vida de Cristo adolescente donde, perfecto humano, fue poco a poco leyendo en las Escrituras el doloroso destino que habría que sufrir. Es un retorno a sus inseguridades, a las tentaciones de huida y a su decisión de aceptarlo por amor.

◊ Los graneros y el olivo eran elementos típicos del paisaje galileo.

◊ «En los recodos», en cada instante de la vida judía estaban presentes, desde la infancia, la Ley y los profetas.

◊ «He escuchado [...] la voz de nuestros padres, a Isaías exultante» hace referencia al aprendizaje y lectura de los profetas, en particular, a los Cantos del Siervo de Isaías, que anuncian su Pasión y Muerte y que, poco a poco, tuvo que ir descubriendo con miedo.

◊ «Quiero madera o la muerte» es Jesús gritando las palabras de Aleixandre en "Unidad en ella" (La destrucción o el amor): «Quiero amor o la muerte». Sin embargo, mientras que el sevillano desea fundirse con el cosmos, Cristo anhela hacer suyo nuestro pecado, representado en la madera.

◊ El haya estaba presente en el Templo de Salomón.

◊ «Ya está aquí la siega» es una frase tomada de Jn 4, 35.

◊ La ceniza es símbolo de penitencia y unión con Dios. Relacionada con ella, el «polvo» se menciona en la imposición de esta al inicio de la Cuaresma: «Acuérdate que eres polvo y en polvo te convertirás».

◊ El ébano, mencionado en Ez 27,15, era una madera lujosa, obtenida a partir del comercio.

◊ La Amada del Cantar de los Cantares era de origen africano.

JESÚS CAE POR PRIMERA VEZ

Donde Jesús se descubre como «sacerdote, víctima y altar»

¿Por qué brilla el sol sedientos rayos,
hay polvo en el camino
pero tiende la oscuridad de fieltro un velo?
Sombra total.

Soy Bartimeo que avanza las pendientes ¿y Ananías?
Ananías no está, hoy no vendrá Ananías,
no será el mundo fuego en manos del profeta
¿no basta ya el ardor de mis entrañas?

Quiero verter en estas piedras
la ira que rebosa el cáliz, mas engendrado
desde el vientre y por los siglos como Siervo
única res, becerro de esperanza
en mi desesperanza y las tinieblas.

«Serán ellos tu pueblo y tú serás su Dios»
pero ¿qué seré yo sino carne maldita,
impenetrable escándalo, celeste libación?

Soy mesa de sacrificio,
ocho lustros de desierto sin memoria
soy la ceguera de Abrahán.
Soy sacerdote eterno,
según el rito de Melquisedec.

JESÚS CAE POR PRIMERA VEZ

Donde Jesús se descubre como «sacerdote, víctima y altar»

No fue fácil cargar de significado, diferenciar, las tres caídas que la tradición popular atribuye a Cristo camino del Calvario. En esta primera, Jesús adhiere a su carne la oscuridad de tantos hombres sin fe, pasando de la angustia por un destino incierto y aparentemente cruel a la aceptación de este. En unos pocos versos se condensa lo que debió de ser su vida: un camino de la incertidumbre a la aceptación, del desconocimiento a la autoconciencia de su condición de «sacerdote, víctima y altar».

Este tema está desarrollado en detalle en la Carta a los Hebreos. Como esta, el poema es rico en referencias a los Textos Sagrados.

◊   Bartimeo es el ciego de Mc 10,46-52.

◊   Ananías fue quien le abrió a San Pablo los ojos en Damasco (Hch 9,11).

◊   «El mundo fuego en manos del profeta» es una evocación a Elías, que hizo descender fuego sobre el altar consagrado al Señor (1Re 18,38).

◊   Como antes, se hace referencia a los Cantos del Siervo de Isaías, aunque aquí ya con un tono más optimista: «ya no tendrás que beber el cáliz de mi ira» (Is 51,22)

◊   Las palabras «becerro de esperanza» evocan el becerro de oro de los israelitas en los «ocho lustros de desierto», tras huir de Egipto. Frente al ídolo, Cristo es la verdadera divinidad.

◊   «La ceguera de Abraham» nos recuerda que también al patriarca le fue exigida confianza total en Dios en varias ocasiones: al prometérsele un hijo y al pedirse su sacrificio.

◊   «Serán ellos tu pueblo y tú serás su Dios» está tomado de Rt 1, 16, libro en el que se abre la puerta de la salvación a los gentiles.

◊   «Soy sacerdote eterno según el rito de Melquisedec» hace referencia al sacerdocio de Cristo desarrollado en Hb 7-9 y evoca las palabras del Sal 110.

JESÚS ENCUENTRA A SU MADRE

Donde Jesús, antes de gritar «a quien podría salvarlo de la muerte» mira a la única criatura capaz de comprenderle

Sécame Madre las lágrimas con tus caricias de lino,
tu olor a rosa,
con el manto que curaba en las aristas nazarenas
mis rodillas de niño ilusionado.

Grito tu abrazo como en las noches sin sueño,
ahora que soy oscuro,
tu abrazo de terciopelo, tu olor a confiado fuego,
a añorado hogar;
tu abrazo aquí al aprender de los maestros,
lo que habría de vivir.

Modelemos juntos con mis lágrimas
en el taller de Nazaret
esta esperanza que no entiendo,
tu confianza peregrina, tu fe nupcial.

 JESÚS ENCUENTRA A SU MADRE

Donde Jesús, antes de gritar «a quien podría salvarlo de la muerte» mira a la única criatura capaz de comprenderle

No hay nada más sencillo que el amor de una madre hacia su hijo. No hay aquí profecías, ni llanto hiperbólico, ni filosofía existencial. Es un instante donde la mirada de María y la de Cristo se fusionan y con sencillez, recuerdan una humanidad plena y corriente.

Esta cuarta estación es Jesús llorando y evocando el lecho materno. Es Jesús volviendo a Nazaret, a «las aristas» a la infancia de desnudas «rodillas de niño ilusionado». Es María abrazando a un hijo débil y enfermo, María que no entiende pero que, como en aquel arrebato de «confianza peregrina» (camino de casa de Isabel) y de «fe nupcial» en Caná, elige–o más bien se le regala–la fe.

◊ El lino hace referencia al texto de Ap 19,7-8 : «han llegado las bodas del Cordero y su esposa se ha engalanado y se le ha concedido vestirse de lino deslumbrante de blancura—el lino son las buenas acciones de los santos».

◊ Son numerosas las referencias al hogar de Nazaret y al deseo unaminiando—y realmente de todos los hombres—de renacer: «aristas nazarenas», «niño ilusionado», «confiado fuego», «taller de Nazaret»…

◊ Del mismo modo, queda latente la humanidad de Jesucristo y su duda: «noches sin sueño / ahora que soy osucro», «esperanza que no entiendo».

◊ El verso «al aprender de los maestros» evoca su episodio de tres días extraviado en Jerusalén, formándose a los pies de los maestros de la Ley (Lc 2,41-50)…¿Estaría ahí formándose Saulo de Tarso?

◊ «Tu fe nupcial» recuerda la fe de María en las Bodas de Caná, primer milagro de Cristo (Jn 2,1-13).

EL CIRENEO AYUDA A JESÚS

Donde Cristo nos recuerda sus palabras de unas horas antes:
«Soy yo quien os ha escogido»

Moisés, el tartamudo y asesino,
recelo en el desierto;
de Jericó vino Rajab;
Saúl en su impaciencia;
el infiel monarca Roboán.
Sara junto a Asmodeo,
un gesareno entre tumbas,
embuste de Galilea.

No ha escogido mi sed
un imperio fastuoso,
ni triunfo púrpura de incienso,
las faces de las monedas
o armadura de metal.
No ha escogido tus manos,
torcidas y callosas,
ni tu pensar vacío;
no tu oro ni el saber,
sino ánforas con hueco:
elegida está tu vida.

Gota a gota quiero
tu esencia de pecado y de pobreza,
tu compañía en mi copa,
aun en tu dormitar
o en tu vivir inquieto,
y una resurrección
en la morada nueva
por mi Padre engalanada.

Y llegará mi Espíritu a tus manos,
cantarás de gozo con sus frutos
en nazarena nube,
en un estático Jordán.
Renacerá del vientre de tu esposa
la Palabra predicada a los gentiles
lágrimas y pasión,
un único brillo de jaspe
esta madera enferma
que cargas con tus ascos en silencio

 # EL CIRENEO AYUDA A JESÚS

Donde Cristo nos recuerda sus palabras de unas horas antes:
«Soy yo quien os ha escogido»

El mérito del Cireneo no reside en sus intentos de ayudar, sino en el haber sido elegido por Jesucristo para una misión. La elección no se sustenta en méritos pasados ni en una excelente condición humana, sino que se realiza gratuitamente en Cristo. Es una elección misericordiosa, liberadora y compartida con tantos otros a lo largo de la historia que, como santos en las vidrieras de una catedral, van apareciendo según se recorre el poema e impregnándolo de su pecado, esperando que Jesús en la Cruz lo lave.

◊ Moisés mató a un capataz egipcio (Ex 2, 12), tartamudeaba (Ex 4, 10) y no pudo entrar en la Tierra Prometida por su desconfianza respecto a Dios en Nm 20, 12.

◊ Rajab era una prostituta de Jericó que refugió espías israelitas y acabó dando culto a Dios (Jos 2, 8-21).

◊ Saúl, el primer rey de Israel, fue rechazado por Dios tras su desobediencia en 1 S 15 1-23, aunque perdonado posteriormente por David (1 S 26).

◊ Roboán, hijo de Salomón, quiso contentar a los hombres antes que al Señor (1 Re 12, 1-24).

◊ Asmodeo, personificación del demonio, se enamora de Sara en Tb 3, 8 y provoca la muerte de sus siete primeros maridos en la noche de bodas.

◊ «Un gesareno entre tumbas» evoca el endemoniado de Mc 5, 1-20.

◊ Pedro es el «embuste de Galilea» y un amante de «armadura de metal».

◊ «Las faces de las monedas» hace referencia al episodio narrado en Mt 22, 15-21,

◊ Las ánforas eran usadas para albergar alimento. En este poema, se usan metafóricamente para hablar de los corazones humanos, destinados a almacenar el amor de Dios.

◊ «Tu compañía en mi copa» es una invitación a compartir el cáliz de Cristo, imagen propia de algunas situaciones del Evangelio (Mt 20, 23 o Lc 22, 42).

◊ «Llegará mi espíritu» en ayuda de tu debilidad, parafraseando Rm 8, 26.

◊ En «cantarás de gozo» caben muchos que han alabado exultantes a Dios a lo largo de toda la Escritura: Ana en 1 S 2, 1-10, María en Lc 1, 46-55, Zacarías en Lc 1, 68-79, San Pablo en Rm 8, 31-39 o FLp 2, 6-11….y también a lo largo de la historia de la Iglesia: San Isidro Labrador, Santa Catalina de Siena, San Francisco de Asís, Santo Domingo de Guzmán, San Juan Pablo II en su espontaniedad de tantas ocasiones….

◊ Tanto la «nazarea nube» como el «estático Jordán» hacen referencia a intervenciones del Espíritu Santo: la primera sobre María en la Concepción de Cristo (Lc 1, 35) y la segunda, al Bautismo del Señor (Lc 3, 22).

◊ «Renacerá del vientre de tu esposa / la palabra predicada a los gentiles» anuncia que la esposa del Cireneo será considerada por San Pablo (el «apóstol de los gentiles») como una madre (Rm 16 ,13).

◊ «Un único brillo de jaspe / esta madera enferma» es una reescritura libre de la lapidaria frase de Ga 6, 14.

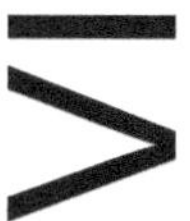

VERÓNICA LIMPIA EL ROSTRO DE JESÚS

Donde muchos años después, una mujer recuerda que una sola mirada cambió su vida

La piedra pasional camino del Calvario
guardaba en sus resquicios los olores de Damasco,
el cántico de las criaturas desnudo por Umbría,
de dos en dos kerigma desde un pueblo de Toulouse.

Fue una aureola limpia su mirada, el Mundo Entero,
el mar, su espuma, cada grano de la playa,
tribulación, el hambre, los pobres y los borrachos,
acariciados por sus ojos de niño fatigado.

Ojos sedientos, conchas profundas con coral,
burbujas de mil súplicas. Y me han mirado.
Me ha mirado su Palabra, soy la samaritana,
como la Magdalena he olido sus sandalias
porque en la tiniebla ha besado mi pobreza

He escuchado su voz en el desierto, en los pliegues
de este lino bendecido, en los espacios de mi piel
su voz de Padre me ha llamado Evodia, Síntique,
Lidia, Marta, Salomé, María, adúltera transformada.

Como Natanael electa debajo de la higuera
fui Zaqueo y gusté su rostro;
miré Canáan y pude entrar en ella
Yo me he encontrado con Cristo.
Con Cristo crucificado
Con Cristo resucitado.

Verónica limpia el rostro de Jesús

Donde muchos años después, una mujer recuerda que una sola mirada cambió su vida

La elección del Cireneo deja aquí paso al encuentro. En un ambiente de leyenda medieval, Verónica–la mujer que limpió a Cristo y encontró en su paño impreso el rostro del Señor–hace una todas las conversiones, pues todas guardan en común lo esencial del encuentro con Jesucristo. Dios concedió a Moisés mirar Caná, la Tierra Prometida antes de morir. Por la muerte y resurrección de Cristo, Verónica ha podido entrar en ella.

◊ El tercer verso hace referencia a San Francisco de Asís, el santo de Umbría que se desnudó delante de su padre para decirle que no quería nada de él y compuso una bellísima alabanza titulada Cántico de las Criaturas.

◊ De su tiempo es también el otro gran fundador medieval, Santo Domingo de Guzmán. A pesar de nacer en Caleruega (Burgos), empezó su obra en Prouille, a 80 km de Toulouse. Desde ahí, empezó a mandar a sus frailes, en grupos de dos, al mundo entero, a formarse y anunciar el kerigma, el Evangelio volviendo a las fuentes, al anuncio pentecostal de Pedro (Hch 2, 14-47).

◊ En «tribulación, el hambre» resuena Rm 8, 35, tan bien traducido al lenguaje popular en la canción Nada nos separará.

◊ La samaritana tiene un encuentro sorprendente con Cristo en Jn 4.

◊ María Magdalena era una prostituta y la primera en ver, según los Evangelios (Jn 11, 20-31), a Cristo resucitado.

◊ Evodia y Síntique fueron las dos primeras cabezas de la Iglesia de Filipos (Flp 4, 2). A pesar de su encuentro con Cristo, guardaban cierta rivalidad.

◊ Como se cuenta en Hc 16, 14-15 Lidia fue la primera en bautizarse, junto a su familia, en esa ciudad.

◊ Marta y María eran las hermanas de Lázaro. Muchas son las veces que le abrieron las puertas de su hogar a Cristo: Lc 10, 38-42, Jn 11, 1-43, Jn 12, 1-8.

◊ Salomé es la madre de los Zebedeos, los apóstoles Santiago el Mayor y Juan (Mt 27, 56).

◊ «Adúltera transformada» habla de la mujer de Jn 8, 1-7, sorprendida en «flagrante adulterio» pero perdonada por Cristo.

◊ «Natanael electa debajo de la higuera» hace referencia a la elección del apóstol Bartolomé (jn 1, 45-50), que pasó de la soberbia a la pobreza de Espíritu.

◊ Zaqueo fue llamado a seguir a Cristo cuando se había subido para espiarle encima de una higuera (Lc 19, 1-10).

◊ Como se ha dicho, Moisés solo pudo mirar Canáan, la Tierra Prometida, como castigo por su desobediencia, como premio por su fidelidad (Dt 34).

◊ El último verso adelanta ya la Resurrección de Cristo, sin la cual no hay esperanza posible.

JESÚS CAE POR SEGUNDA VEZ

Donde Jesús toma la carne de los enfermos, solitarios y moribundos

Hoy vienen a mí todas las vendas de la historia
unge su enfermedad mi piel;
hoy me embalsaman la lepra, la peste y la depresión.
nadie eleva mi camilla al Cielo
o un «Talita Kum» caliente y esperanzado,
«Lázaro despierta» …y a mí, ¿quién me hará despertar?

En la trampa me rodea la red del cazador,
vierte en mí el pecado sus efectos
sangre de bilis amarga, no hay punto sin dolor.
Soy de cerebro seco y ahora la soledad.

Enfermo muero en una cama de hospital vacía,
en piso de telarañas,
en el estiércol del mundo y la inmundicia de Calcuta.
No hay entierro ni luto.
Frío y dolor.

Hoy sois ese leproso sirio,
y la sangre de mi promesa guarda
las aguas del Jordán.

JESÚS CAE POR SEGUNDA VEZ

Donde Jesús toma la carne de los enfermos, solitarios y moribundos

Durante todo el Antiguo Testamento, los reyes, sacerdotes y profetas eran ungidos con óleos para ayudarles a cumplir con su misión. La unción que Cristo–cuyo nombre en griego, Χριστος, significa ungido–recibe es la de la enfermedad y el sufrimiento humanos.

El poema es el delirio de Jesús en su agonía. En su cabeza se mezclan recuerdos de curaciones. Su muerte, como el más pobre de los pobres, purifica la vida de los hombres como Naamán, «ese leproso sirio» que quedó limpio al bañarse en el Jordán.

◊ La lepra era una enfermedad muy habitual en tiempos de Jesús, la peste en la Edad Media y la depresión, en la actualidad.

◊ «Nadie eleva mi camilla al cielo» es el recuerdo, por parte de Cristo, del paralítico al que sus amigos llevaron a Cristo haciendo un boquete en el techo (Mc 2, 14-16).

◊ «Un "Talita Kum" caliente y esperanzado» hace referencia a la curación de la hija de Jairo (Mc 5, 41).

◊ «Lázaro despierta» evoca la resurrección de Lázaro narrada en Jn 11, 1-43.

◊ «La red del cazador» y «no hay punto sin dolor» son frases, respectivamente, de Sal 38, 17.

◊ «La inmundicia de Calcuta» es un claro guiño a Madre Teresa.

◊ La historia de Naamán, «ese leproso sirio» que fue curado al bañarse en el Jordán se narra en 2R 5, 1-13. La sangre de Cristo, bajo la Nueva Alianza, la promesa definitiva, cumple el mismo papel purificador que las aguas del Jordán. La curación que ofrece es tan fácil para los hombres y tan poco espectacular que, a muchos, como a Naamán, les parece demasiado sencilla.

Jesús consuela a las mujeres de Jerusalén

Donde el Espíritu nos convence «de pecado, justicia y juicio»

No lloréis mis costras
sedimento de pecado y manantial de gracia,
ni mis llagas, mi fiebre y mi desmayo.
Quítate Jerusalén el luto,
no malgastes Antioquía tu mortaja.

No hay parturienta triste ni noche sin sus grillos,
llorad la higuera seca,
al rico de Judea, a Epulón en su soberbia,
al agrietado barro que no se deja modelar.
Llorad al acebuche sin injertos
a la mañana fría que no quiere nacer.

Llorad, llorad, orad sin tregua,
no me duele el pecado ni la blasfemia caprichosa,
me duelen las corazas,
los odres polvorientos, la esclerosis de comprar
a mi Padre con las obras.

Desgarrada la espalda, mis rodillas rotas,
el odio ha cincelado mis fisuras;
mis huesos cuento,
en su crujir Caín levanta,
y con él Rajab, Gómer, Dalila,
la ira, la envida y la soberbia,
todo se ha perdonado, solo una gota basta
una sola gota de la sangre de mis manos.

JESÚS CONSUELA A LAS MUJERES DE JERUSALÉN

Donde el Espíritu nos convence «de pecado, justicia y juicio»

La pasión de Cristo es el acto más doloroso de la historia: por sus venas pasó cada gota de dolor sufrida por la humanidad a lo largo de los siglos. Pero a la vez, es el acto de amor más grande: al querer morir por todos, Jesús abre gratuitamente las puertas del Cielo a quienes quieren acogerlo. No hay otra vía de salvación que la aceptación de este regalo.

El llanto de la octava estación son las lágrimas invisibles de Cristo por Jerusalén–las mismas de Mt 23, 37-39–y no las de Jerusalén por Cristo. Es el gemido desesperado de quien sabe que existe gente que, en su soberbia, no querrá nunca acoger su duro sacrificio. En medio de la mayor de las agonías, Jesús nos recuerda que no son nuestras acciones ni nuestros méritos, ni siquiera su imitación, quienes nos llevarán al Cielo, sino únicamente su sangre.

◊   En el verso segundo, «manantial de gracia» evoca Is 41, 18 y Jn 7, 38.

◊   En «Quítate Jerusalén el luto» se oyen las palabras de Is 60 y la canción engendrada a partir de ella, Jerusalén, quítate el velo de tristeza.

◊   «No malgastes Antioquía tu mortaja» adelanta los mártires que verá la ciudad a lo largo de todo el siglo I.

◊   «No hay parturienta triste» es una transcripción libre de Jn 16,21.

◊   La «higuera seca» de Mc 13, 28-31 no quiso acoger a Cristo y renovarse.

◊   Tampoco quisieron el rico de Mt 19, 16-26, que quería salvarse en sus obras ni el derrochador de Lc 16, 19-31, a quien la tradición ha nombrado Epulón.

◊   El «agrietado barro que no se deja modelar» lleva de nuevo a Jr 18. En la imagen se incluyen todos los que, en su soberbia, no quieren dejar que la salvación de Cristo cambie sus vidas.

◊   El «acebuche sin injertos» es, en Rm 11, 16-24, todo que no quiere que entre en él la savia fresca que representa Jesucristo y sigue confiando en la salvación por las obras de la Ley.

◊   En los «odres polvorientos» no cabe vino nuevo (LC 5, 33-39).

◊   Los tres primeros versos de la última estrofa reescriben secciones del Sal 22.

◊   Rajab y Gómer son prostitutas y Dalila, la mujer que hizo caer a Sansón.

◊   En los últimos versos laten los acordes de Madre (Estación XIII) de Hakuna: «Sólo con su sangre volveremos a nacer / con la sangre de Jesús de Nazaret».

JESÚS CAE POR TERCERA VEZ

Donde Jesús, hecho pecado sin conocerlo, toma la carne del hijo pródigo y sueña desde el suelo con la casa de su Padre

¿Cuándo verán mis ojos los viñedos nuevos
de tu casa, Padre; y empaparán las azucenas,
del Líbano la flor y el canto de la tórtola
mi contorno deformado en tu perfil redondo?

Quiero volver, sesenta estadios faltan,
hasta alcanzar mis pies tu huerto y su espesura
lavar mi piel leprosa y olvidar
mi perfume de burdel, el tinte de algarroba.

¿Cuándo poder decir, ya sea entre criados,
que he vuelto a tus umbrales, a tu útero caliente?
Mi hermano junto a mí abraza mis heridas,
una observancia pura curando mi adulterio.

¿O acaso un día Padre, vendrás a recogerme?
Aborto sangriento soy, por tierra derramado
el gusano del Pecado coloniza mis arterias
y en el suelo dislocado mi paladar es seca teja.

¡Llévame contigo Padre, álzame del polvo
donde se arrastra la serpiente! Que el barro de mi piel
moldee las vasijas y mi sangre en el banquete
sea la ardiente llama de la leña que te cargo.
Los convidados listos, vienen de los caminos,
una sola cosa falta ¿ves Padre, tú, el Cordero?

JESÚS CAE POR TERCERA VEZ

Donde Jesús, hecho pecado sin conocerlo, toma la carne del hijo pródigo y sueña desde el suelo con la casa de su Padre

En esta tercera caída, Jesús bebe las gotas más amargas de su plena condición humana, La tentación y todas las consecuencias del pecado le visitan. Es el percador por excelencia, el hijo pródigo que, de vuelta a casa, se encuentra exhausto, caído en el camino. Cristo es aquí todos los que quieren de nuevo experimentar la misericordia del Padre. En un estado rayano la locura y la oscuridad de quienes nada les queda en la vida, recuerda el hogar y los momentos de felicidad. Una evocación que termina sugiriendo, en el párrafo final, la gran contradicción y tentación de su vida: saber que su misión era sufrir para dar vida al Mundo.

◊ La flor del Líbano, símbolo de eternidad, es una imagen constante a lo largo de todo el Antiguo Testamento.

◊ «El canto de la tórtola» anuncia en Ct 2, 12 el verano, el tiempo de cosechar, donde Amado y Amada se unirán definitivamente.

◊ Frente al contorno deformado de los hombres, el «perfil redondo» de Dios.

◊ «Sesenta estadios» era la distancia que separaba Emaús de Jerusalén, espacio más que suficiente para un encuentro con Cristo.

◊ «Su huerto y su espesura» es un guiño al Cántico Espiritual B de San Juan de la Cruz.

◊ «Seca teja» evoca la sed agónica de Sal 22, 16.

◊ «El polvo donde se arrastra la serpiente» hace referencia al castigo de Gn 3,14.

◊ «Las vasijas» son de nuevo una referencia a Jr 18.

◊ «La leña que te cargo» es la Cruz, donde se «prenderá fuego al Mundo» (Lc 12, 49), donde se castigarán los pecados de la humanidad.

◊ La pregunta final «¿ves Padre, tú, el Cordero?» es la misma que Isaac, inocente, le dirige a su padre Abrahán en Gn 22, 7. Cristo, humano, tiene tentaciones de huir de su destino, aunque como en el huerto, acaba aceptando el cáliz.

 # JESÚS DESPOJADO DE SUS VESTIDURAS

Donde María contempla el cuerpo que salió de sus entrañas.
Donde al fin Dios se nos muestra «cara a cara»

En Belén también hacía frío,
el frío de los astros y el silencio de los montes.
José me dio su manto, tu hoy nos das tu sangre
que por tu cuerpo fluye, por tu desnudo cuerpo.
Cedro también se olía entre las pajas del establo.

Quiero abrazar una vez más tu cuerpo abierto,
el río de tus venas que acaricia pecadores,
mapa de la Subura y plano de las prisiones,
desesperanza en planta que embriaga tu ternura.

No caben en tu piel más agujeros
tu vida escapa, el Pneuma se derrama,
al mirarte profetizan y los ancianos sueñan,
se postran las naciones.

Aquí está la puerta, la estrecha puerta,
el Pastor, la vid, serpiente en el desierto;
cinco llagas y dos peces tejen
al rasgarse, los colores disgregados en Babel.

Cinco llagas en un cuerpo ázimo y humano,
reunidas para siempre doce tribus.
Cinco llagas y una mirada basta
de Levante a Occidente y hasta la Reina del Sur.

En Belén también hubo extranjeros
y desgraciados pastores, indigentes y malditos.
En Belén también te vi llorar desnudo
mas hoy ha sido revelado tu misterio:
Moisés al fin se ha levantado el velo.

JESÚS DESPOJADO DE SUS VESTIDURAS

Donde María contempla el cuerpo que salió de sus entrañas.
Donde al fin Dios se nos muestra «cara a cara»

La humanidad de Cristo es aún algo demasiado inabarcable en el siglo XXI. Ni el racionalismo de la crítica histórica ni las figuras de Jesús-obrero o Cristo-guerrillero encierran una mínima parte de su misterio. Jesucristo es un hombre débil, absurdo y desnudo, pero solo a través de su carne–real y enferma como la nuestra–podemos contemplar al Padre. De otro modo Dios queda relegado a un concepto, a ideas manipulables y nuestra existencia, a un juego absurdo. Es en la desnudez de Cristo donde la carne humana dignifica su condición. Es en la Eucaristía, que los versos finales del poema evocan, donde Jesús, Dios hecho hombre, viene a nuestro encuentro y nos salva.

◊ El poema tiene una estructura encuadrada, con Belén al inicio y al final, como tan dulcemente intuía Manolo Escobar «soy amor en el pesebre y sufrimiento en la cruz».

◊ Dos tipos de realezas contrastan, el «cedro» del principio, madera real israelí y la desnudez y el sinsentido de la Cruz del final.

◊ «El frío de los astros y el silencio de los montes» son palabras literales del rezo de Completas.

◊ La Subura era el barrio popular y mala fama de la Roma antigua.

◊ El «Pneuma» es en la Escritura el spolo de vida del Espíritu.

◊ Los ancianos que «sueñan» y «profetizan» son Simeón y Ana (Lc 2, 33-38).

◊ «Se postran las naciones» recuerda el Sal 71.

◊ La «puerta estrecha», el «Pastor», la «vid» son palabras que el propio Cristo refiere a sí mismo en distintas partes del Evangelio.

◊ Los que miraran «la serpiente en el desierto» puesta por Moisés sobre su báculo quedaban sanados (Nm 21,9).

◊ En el último verso de la quinta estrofa resuenan Lc 13, 29 y Mt 12, 42.

◊ Los «extranjeros de Belén» son los Magos de Oriente.

◊ «Moisés al fin se ha levantado el velo» hace referencia a Ex 34, 34. El patriarca tenía que cubrirse la cara con un velo en presencia de Dios, pero ahora los cristianos miraremos a Dios al contemplar el cuerpo desnudo de Cristo.

Jesús es clavado en la cruz

*Donde tres promesas de Cristo nos adhieren con clavos a Él
en la vida y tras la muerte*

Llegará un día en que el Nilo
no ensanche más su cauce
y tornarán las ranas, los piojos y langostas;
el gallo a medianoche resplandor de las vergüenzas
y en Ramá, Raquel será un aullido
sus lágrimas que caen por quienes nunca llorarán.

Volverá a picar tu corazón el águila
y te arrebatará el olvido y el perdón,
tu candidez manchada,
despierto aún vagando sin aceite que velar.
Serás David a Urías, Jonás bajo el ricino
corrupta sabiduría en manos de Salomón.

Pero hoy un trueno ha abierto el cielo
y del estiércol brota la Rosa de Sarón,
la brisa en la ventana y el rocío,
nacido de lo alto, hoy nos visita el Sol.

Porque estaré contigo, allí donde te muevas,
Malta en tempestades, perfume en el dolor,
cuando al andar el fuego prenda tu alimento
o seas sal que pierda su sabor.

Donde la vida como torre
piedra a piedra derretida y en la espesura oculta
como aguijón de acero clavado en tus anhelos,
en la melancolía, el desempleo y el estrés.
Donde el sentido, ese invisible soplo
desaparezca para nunca retornar.

En tu pobreza, en tu pecado, en tu desesperado grito
Ella estará contigo. Tú estarás conmigo.

 # JESÚS ES CLAVADO EN LA CRUZ

Donde tres promesas de Cristo nos adhieren con clavos a Él en la vida y tras la muerte

Aun en medio de la crueldad, el abandono y el absurdo, emerge la belleza. Tres frases de Cristo—«Mujer, ahí tienes a tu madre» (Jn 19, 26), «Hijo, ahí tienes a tu madre» (Jn 19, 27), «Te aseguro que hoy estarás conmigo en el paraíso» (Lc 23, 43)– nos unen para siempre con Él, su Padre y el Espíritu. Por su muerte y su resurrección, se hace presente en cada momento de nuestra vida, sin importar nuestra condición, y nos invita a vivenciarlo.

◊ Que el Nilo «no ensanche más su cauce» signiicaba sequía y hambruna en el Antiguo Egipto.

◊ «Las ranas, los piojos y langostas» son algunas de las plagas de Ex 7-12.

◊ «El gallo a medianoche resplandor de las vergüenzas» hace referencia a la triple negación de Pedro.

◊ «En Ramá, Raquel será un aullido» son palabras de Jr 31, 15, donde una madre llora sus hijos perdidos.

◊ En la mitología griega, un águila le comía el hígado a Prometeo, representación de la soberbia, cada noche.

◊ En «despierto aún vagando sin aceite que velar» resuena la parábola de las diez vírgenes (Mt 25, 1-13).

◊ David mandó a Urías al frente para acostarse con su mujer, Jonás se rebeló bajo un ricino contra Dios por no incendiar Nínive y Salomón, a pesar de la sabiduría recibida, fue detrás de otros dioses (1R 11, 9-13).

◊ En el Bautismo del Señor también se abrió el cielo (Mt 16, 16-17).

◊ La rosa de Sarón es una imagen del Amado (Dios) del capítulo 2 del Cantar de los Cantares.

◊ Dios se le presenta a Elías como «suave brisa» (1 Re 19, 12).

◊ «Nacido de lo alto, hoy nos visita el Sol» es una frase invertida del Benedictus (Lc 1, 68-79), que anuncia la llegada del Mesías esperado y es muy leído en los albores de la Navidad.

◊ El barco de San Pablo encuentra milagrosamente Malta tras una tempestad (Hch 28).

◊ «Sal que pierda su sabor» evoca las palabras de Mt 5, 13.

◊ «En la espesura oculta» entronca con el Cántico Espiritual B de San Juan de la Cruz.

◊ En 2Co 12, 7, San Pablo habla de un «aguijón» clavado en su carne, causa de sus sufrimientos.

◊ El «desesperado grito» es el de la humanidad, asumido por Cristo en la Cruz.

◊ Los últimos versos son la reescritura de las tres frases sobre las que gira el poema.

JESÚS MUERE EN LA CRUZ

*Donde no hay palabras para expresar este milagro de Amor
tan infinito*

Ecce Homo
Aquí está el hombre.

Yace en una Cruz abandonado,
en el fragor de este llover caliente y sudoroso,
un Cordero roto, tal fundida vela;
promesa de vapor en los destierros.
¿por qué sabe el amor tan frío?
¿Quién hizo de carne el nuevo Arca?
Yace un loco sin sentido,
la soberbia, la lujuria, el egoísmo,
ira, pereza, envidia, gula,
del negro de Quedar la sangre del Esposo.

Aquí Diluvio y Sodoma
las guerras y las bombas, los lamentos de las viudas,
los que no huyeron a Egipto ni embarcaron en el Nilo.
Aquí una madre llora una grieta abierta,
por los peldaños del templo el sacerdocio escurre
de la barba de Aarón lo beben las naciones.

Ante el silencio de Dios, aquí está su respuesta.

JESÚS MUERE EN LA CRUZ

*Donde no hay palabras para expresar este milagro de Amor
tan infinito*

Si en poemas anteriores han acompañado la Virgen, Verónica
o el propio Cristo, aquí nadie habla. «¡Qué solos se quedan
los muertos!» reza la *Rima LXXIII* de Bécquer. La estación
pinta un paisaje lluvioso y muerto que acompañan al lector
hasta el último verso, en el que puede condensarse todo el
misterio del cristianismo: «Ante el silencio de Dios, aquí está
su respuesta». ¿Dónde está Dios cuando se muere un niño?
¿Dónde está cuando los hombres luchan y cuando en las
UCIs solo huele a muerto? Aquí está su hijo. Sufriendo con
los que quedan, sufriendo lo de los que quedan.

◊ El «Ecce Homo» pronunciado por Pilato en Jn 19, 5 se coloca aquí. Como en todo el Viacrucis, el tiempo y el espacio son curvos y de contornos difusos, los santos y profetas se abrazan libremente, como supongo, sucederá en la Eternidad.

◊ El «llover caliente y sudoroso» es un recurso estético clásico (véase, por ejemplo, Germinal de Zola), pero también símbolo de salvación en Is 55, 10.

◊ Cristo, «Cordero roto» es el Cordero Pascual definitivo. Es también el «nuevo Arca», el de la Alianza definitiva, pues Él ha pagado el castigo de todos los que la incumplan.

◊ Se mencionan los siete pecados capitales: «la soberbia, la lujuria, el egoísmo / ira, pereza, envidia, gula».

◊ «Del negro de Quedar» tiene la piel la novia del Cantar de los Cantares y su Esposo es Cristo.

◊ «Aquí Diluvio y Sodoma» indican de nuevo que en Jesús se realiza el castigo definitivo.

◊ «Los que no huyeron a Egipto» hace referencia a los Santos Inocentes (Mt 2, 13-18).

◊ Moisés fue quien «embarcó en el Nilo (Ex 2, 1-10).

◊ Al morir Cristo el velo del Templo se rasgó en dos. Desde ese momento, «el sacerdocio escurre» y Dios se hace accesible al mundo entero (Mt 27,51).

◊ En «de la barba de Aarón lo beben las naciones» resuena el Sal 133.

JESÚS DESCENDIDO DE LA CRUZ Y PUESTO EN BRAZOS DE SU MADRE

Donde ahora es María quien mira a Jesús

Hoy el viento se ha secado y las estrellas
han dejado de brillar,
la nieve envuelve una capa de primavera
y ha dejado tu cuerpo,
la carne que cuidé sin poseer y que ahora abrazo,
hecho seco erial,
como Masá y Meribá, huesos sin soplo,
lugar sin vida.

No cobijarán nunca los siglos un dolor más grande
que el presente,
grito como Noemí lo que no puedes ya decir
bailan las jambas del templo,
tiembla el abismo.

Con mis dedos rozo el amor de tus ojeras,
la predicación de tu sonrisa
y tus pies de mensajero y mi talón mordido.

Sueño que vives
que vuelve tu locura a escandalizar las calles
mientras da Paz.
Quiero volver a verte caído en las pendientes,
en el taller,
perdido entre los doctores, tu risa de dulce fuego.
Quiero alabar contigo en lenguas,
tallar en el madero una rosa de dulzura.

Hágase otra vez Caná de Galilea y que las zarzas
tejan tupidas redes
y no entendamos tus caminos.
Que cante mi alma de nuevo tu grandeza y tu perdón
y recoger las lágrimas
de tu marchito rostro y florecer un Cielo Nuevo
al borde del camino, entre las zarzas;
un árbol de mostaza
para quienes han lavado su inmundicia con tu sangre.

JESÚS DESCENDIDO DE LA CRUZ Y PUESTO EN BRAZOS DE SU MADRE

Donde ahora es María quien mira a Jesús

Como un espejo, María le devuelve a Jesús la mirada que le dirigió camino del Calvario. Es una mirada oscura, pero a la que le ha sido dada la gracia de la fe. Es quizás en el momento de abrazar el cuerpo de su Hijo, inmersa en abismos que nunca experimentaremos, cuando María hace el mayor acto de fe de su existencia. Junto a las venas aún calientes del que llamaron Maestro y Mesías y del que nada queda, Dios le concede la gracia de renovar el *sí* de Nazaret.

◊ En el libro de Rut, Noemí ve morir a su esposo y a sus dos hijos.

◊ «Bailan las jambas del templo», tomado del Auto de Resurrección de Ana Lorite, es una descripción plástica del temblor descrito en Mt 27,51.

◊ «Tus pies de mensajero» y «mi talón moriddo» hacen referencia, respectivamente, a las promesas mesiánicas de Is 52, 7 y el anciano Simeón (Lc 2, 33-35).

◊ La alabanza en lenguas es un don del Espíritu Santo descrito en Is 28,11 o Hch 2,5 y es una de las formas más altas de alabanza y contemplación.

◊ La «rosa de dulzura» hace referencia a la rosa de Pallerols, que animó a San Josemaría a continuar rumbo a Andorra.

◊ «Que cante mi alma de nuevo tu grandeza y tu perdón» es una referencia al Magníficat (Lc 1, 46-50). Es en la fe en Jesucristo de donde salen las más bellas alabanzas. María experimenta aquí, más si cabe que en Nazaret, sus anhelos de alabar.

◊ La zarza es un símbolo contradictorio: Dios se manifestó a Moisés en una «zarza» ardiendo (Ex 2, 3-4), pero también algo que no deja crecer la buena semilla en la parábola del Sembrador (Mc 4, 1-9).

◊ El «árbol de mostaza» evoca la parábola de Lc 13, 18-19.

JESÚS ES SEPULTADO

Dónde la Iglesia, junto a María en el sepulcro, aguarda la segunda Venida de Cristo

Ahora el amor inunda el Mundo,
la espera ha cobrado sentido
y visto nuestros ojos lo soñado por Abrahán;
soñar es realidad,
tus curvos senderos en un punto,
el ascensor a ti, un ascensor de carne,
un indefenso cuerpo en medio de la noche,
un cadáver frío en la piedra del sepulcro.

No existe ya el tiempo,
todo es esperanza, una crisálida en la rama,
la belleza entre nosotros.
¿Podrá acaso el invierno
ennegrecer las hojas del arbusto
o hacer temblar los encinares castellanos?
¿Podrá acaso el dolor corroer de nuevo
si nuestra piel es la de Cristo
y en la suya nuestros nombres tatuados?
¿Podrá algún día la cizaña espesa
sembrar la destrucción entre tus hijos
—bañados en tu sangre de Cordero—
con Espíritu de espera, en una Iglesia abierta?

La alondra al fin ha despertado.

JESÚS ES SEPULTADO

Dónde la Iglesia, junto a María en el sepulcro, aguarda la segunda Venida de Cristo

El Sábado Santo, la decimocuarta estación es un día de fe y espera. Es María junto al sepulcro. Es la Iglesia en silencio recogida en el Carmelo. Esperar es confiar en la oscuridad, confiar sin certezas (Rm 4, 18) y sobre todo, anhelar lo que se espera. La vida nueva que estos versos vislumbran no está basada en seguridades humanas, sino en la fe que ha sido regalada gratuitamente a los que esperan, a los que desean una Vida Nueva.

◊ «Lo soñado por Abrahán» es una evocación de las palabras de Cristo en Jn 8, 56.

◊ En «un ascensor de carne» se evoca el deseo de Santa Teresita de Lisieux, «demasiado pequeña para subir la ruda escalera de la perfección», de elevarse hacia Jesús.

◊ La «crisálida en la rama», de las más brillantes analogías de Santa Teresa, se evoca en su Quinta Morada.

◊ «Nuestra piel es la de Cristo» cuando se escuchan las palabras de Ef 4, 24.

◊ En Is 49,16, Dios reconoce tener nuestros nombres «tatuados» en su palma.

◊ La «cizaña espesa» es conocida, de la parábola de Mt 13, 24-30.

◊ «Bañados en la sangre del Cordero» es reproducción de Ap 7,14 donde se describe así a todos los salvados.

◊ La «Iglesia abierta» retoma la esperanza y la alegría de Is 54,2, que nos invita a la apertura.

◊ La «alondra» avisaba a Romeo y Julieta de la llegada del alba. María ve aquí acercarse un Cielo Nuevo.

La resurección de Jesús

*Donde nuestra carne mortal experimenta ya a Cristo
resucitado*

Se alegra en ti mi corazón, Señor,
porque has tomado tu mi ser.
Soy los denarios de la viuda,
has mirado la roca desechada,
gratis comparto tus manjares,
¿quién me condenará?

Alabaré tu nombre por los días
y tu fidelidad de la vida a la tarde.
El Valle del Loto cruzamos abrazados
y tañen de alegría mis entrañas,
gozoso vuelo,
al rebosar mi copa.

Sostiene mi vida tu presencia,
en el dolor y el sufrimiento
tus acciones bendicen
mi desdichada carne;
obras no necesito,
y tú no quieres sacrificios.

Tu bondad eterna alimenta mi alegría,
Desaparece el pecado;
tuyo soy, Señor, transparente
y rebautizado,
glorioso y resucitado.

Adoro tu cariño y tu atención sincera
adoro en mi tu palpitar,
adoro la hermosura en tu Palabra
Verdad, Amor, Justicia y Paz.

Vocearán las piedras
que la viña ha florecido,
que en mi corazón has susurrado el trigo,
que a quien convences de justicia,
de juicio y de pecado,
le dejas entrar.

Hoy has venido, Señor, a nuestro pueblo,
tu sangre nuestras vidas ha sanado,
Ya no te marcharás.

LA RESURECCIÓN DE JESÚS

Donde nuestra carne mortal experimenta ya a Cristo resucitado

La alegría de la Resurrección toma aquí forma en un cántico de reminiscencias sálmicas, pero donde se dejan entrever también jolglorios como el del Magnificat (Lc 1, 46-54) o el archiconocido canto de los israelitas al pasar el Mar Rojo (Ex 15, Mi fuerza y mi poder es el Señor). Cristo ha resucitado y las puertas del Cielo han sido abiertas para todo el que quiera acogerle. Estamos llamados a una vida nueva en Cristo, que se hace real en cada momento de nuestras vidas.

◊ «Los denarios de la viuda» citan el pasaje de Lc 21, 1-4, en el que Jesús alaba la pequeña ofrenda de una viuda, porque ha entregado todo lo que tenía.

◊ «La roca desechada» de Sal 118, 22, se convierte, por Cristo en piedra angular.

◊ El Valle de Beraca fue el escenario de la victoria de Josafat sobre Moab y Amón.

◊ «Tu no quieres sacrificios ni ofrendas» reza el Sal 51, en línea con el último verso de la tercera estrofa.

◊ «Verdad, Amor, Justicia y Paz» se entremezclan en el Sal 85.

◊ «La viña ha florecido» toma imágenes clásicas del Cantar de los Cantares.

◊ En Jn 16, 8-11, se explica que el Espíritu Santo convencentrá, «de justicia, de juicio y de pecado».